The Mediumship & Psychic Art of

SANDY INGHAM

By
James Christie

With love always,

Sandy

x

ASSMPI and The Otherside Press
Present

The Mediumship & Psychic Art of
SANDY INGHAM

Originally published in 2011 by Mage Publishing.

Revised second edition published by The Otherside Press, 2017.

ISBN: 978-1-909439-99-3

Covers, book design by Susan Tiemann, Interior artwork and photos courtesy Sandy Ingham except where noted.

TOSPBOOKS.COM

Introduction and Author's Note

I first met Sandy Ingham in the spring of 2009 at The Marriott Hotel in Portsmouth. This was at a time in my life when I was promoting and acting as tour manager for Stephen Holbrook, one of Britain's most gifted spiritualist mediums. Portsmouth was one of our premier venues and because I had lots of pleasant memories of the town going back to the 1970s it was a place that I always looked forward to revisiting.

On this particular evening Stephen brought along a new friend and was highly enthusiastic about her talents. She was, he said, a psychic artist who had the ability to sketch the faces of people who had passed over and who were trying to make contact with their loved ones.

Initially, although I tried to keep an open mind, I admit to being just a little bit sceptical. I had come across a number of psychic artists in the past whose work was so crude that very few people, if anyone at all, could identify their sketches and when somebody *did* cautiously accept that the artist's drawing contained a passing likeness to their loved one on the other side, I suspected that there was a degree of self-delusional wish fulfillment going on. After all, people do find it very easy to believe what they want to believe.

If this sounds cruel I make no apology. I have spent all of my adult life in the company of mediums and mystics – I've photographed them, investigated them and have written books about them and in my opinion for every genuine medium out there. There are a hundred who would lay claim to having this ability when they simply do *not* have it – and there are another thousand on top of that who would love to think that they *might* have the gift.

I admit that I am a contradiction. On the one hand, I would be happy to describe myself as a spiritualist but at the same time I am both a cynic and a sceptic. I do not think that this is a bad thing because before I can accept a claim to be true I have to test it, look at it all ways against the middle, apply some suspicion and investigation; I am Doubting Thomas, unable to take something at its face value or someone at their word. I need to put my hand into the wound of Christ. The result is that when I *do* come to a conclusion and form an opinion, it is based on hard evidence taken from serious investigation and not just the psychological convenience of blind faith or wishful thinking.

On that first meeting in Portsmouth I didn't have much of an opportunity to talk to Sandy at any length, but I did see that her presence in the room caused quite a stir. During the first half of Stephen Holbrook's demonstration she sat at a small table to one side of the podium and worked away quietly at her sketches. She also worked very quickly and by the time Stephen had finished the first half of the evening she had completed half a dozen drawings... She did the same again during the second half of the demonstration.

It was obvious from the reaction of the audience, both during the interval and at the end of the night, that her artwork found its mark. When I covertly inspected her pictures, they were all etched in the same style, some more detailed than others, all with a naive and innocent quality that caught the eye and demanded attention. While some of the portraits were not identified, the majority of the pictures were claimed by members of Stephen's audience as being a clear depiction of a lost loved one. There seemed to be no correlation between those who had received a verbal message from Stephen during the evening and those finding a picture of a dead relative.

Sandy made no effort to sell or "push" her artwork, simply asking for a small donation if someone found a picture that they could connect with. There was an option on offer to have a proper portrait produced from the sketch which was a service she did charge for, but here again this was in the small print of her publicity and it was not pushed at all. I remember thinking at the time that if I were her business manager I'd be pushing it like blazes – but that's just me!

Interestingly enough, there was one picture in Sandy's collection that I found beguilingly attractive, so I dropped a couple of quid in her collection box and took my A4 sketch home for further study. Over the last three years I've looked at this picture long and hard… and it's a weird thing. I have no idea who the picture is of – it depicts a sallow faced man, apparently in his thirties, with a goatee beard and hooded eyes. He is wearing a cap and is drawn staring into the distance – and yet I *know* this man. I have never met him in this life, but that does not mean that I haven't met him in a past life or that I might not meet him some time in my future. It is an unsettling picture because it touches something within the core of my soul that cannot be easily identified.

I saw Sandy work on two other occasions over that year and I remember thinking that she would make a marvellous subject for a book. For one thing, there is not a lot of literature on psychic art and for another, unlike a clairvoyant who can always claim that his or her message has got lost in translation because no one in the room could understand it, the psychic artist has got nowhere to hide. If she gets it right she is seen to get it right but if she gets it wrong, then she is seen to get it wrong.

Therefore, when I was approached with the proposition of writing a book about Sandy Ingham I jumped at the chance. I knew that her life story would make interesting (if sometimes harrowing) reading as a standalone biography and I also felt that putting Sandy's artwork side by side with the photographs of the people she was drawing would offer convincing evidence for post mortem survival.

It is inevitable that in a work of this nature a few things slip through the net, especially when one is reviving memories and recollections from 40 or 50 years ago. In the event of any omissions or inaccuracies these are entirely the fault of the author and not of Sandy and the many other people who have contributed their time and memory to the creation of this work.

My thanks go out to my wife Joanna for her tireless support, to Michael Ingham who has given rare insights as to what it is like to live with a lady like Sandy, to the nice people at Mage Publishing and, of course, to Sandy herself for her candour and commitment to this project.

James Christie
York 2011

Please visit Sandy's website at
www.sandyingham.co.uk

One: Born in a Storm

1947 brought one of the worst winters recorded since records began and in the High Peak area of Derbyshire it was particularly bad. The snow fall had been heavy throughout the season and by November huge swathes of the county were cut off from the outside world. In this part of England many properties were still powered by gas and mantle and luxuries like private telephones were very few and far between. Such as they were, most of the phone and power lines were down and heavy drifts made most of the minor roads impassable.

On the morning of November 25th an icy blizzard blasted across the county – thick flakes of snow driven horizontally by an angry wind that rattled window pains and shrieked around the peaks like a demented banshee. To expectant young mother Doreen Williamson most of the storm went unnoticed as she perspired and uttered a few shrieks of her own, labouring away in the process of giving birth to her first child. Given what was to come later it was most curious that she decided to call her daughter Sandra – which is, of course, an abbreviation of Cassandra, who was one of the greatest seers and psychics of the ancient world.

And so, Sandra Williamson greeted the world with a welcome cry at 8 o'clock on a wild November morning, born in the middle of one of the worst storm blizzards in living memory. Neither Doreen nor her husband Reuben, and certainly not little Sandra, had any idea that in many cultures across the planet the nature of a person's birth can be a clear indication of that person's pathway through life. Looking back over that life now, the subject of this book smiles somewhat ruefully and admits that if she had a stormy birth then her subsequent life pathway has had more than its fair share of tempests, typhoons and hurricanes.

Sandy has some happy memories of her childhood and reminisces about her first school, St George's primary, in the village of New Mills which she attended for four years before moving up to Spring Bank Secondary Modern, also in New Mills. And yet, while one cannot contest Sandy's claim of it being a happy childhood, by anybody's standards, it was far from being a "normal" one.

Sandy's happiness came primarily from her relationship with her father. Reuben Williamson was a quarryman by day and a musician by night. Most of the weekday evenings would be taken up with practice sessions and rehearsals leading to a regular weekend concert performed by the Thornsett Brass Band. Reuben was capable of playing most of the instruments in the band but specialized in the euphonium. He was well over six feet tall and towered above the heads of the other musicians. Sandy always felt very proud of her father and she attended many of the concerts he took part in. This provided her hearing with a degree of subliminal training. She learned how to separate the sounds of each individual instrument which was to stand her in good stead, albeit in a different theatre, a little later on in life.

Reuben's jovial conviviality and larger than life personality was in no small way countered by the personality and demeanour of his wife. Doreen had been very young when she'd married Reuben and when it came to the facts of life, especially the biological facts, she was both naïve and ignorant. Quite late in her pregnancy she was talking with her doctor and wanted to know how the baby she was carrying would finally get out of her body. The doctor, in some degree of shock, laconically replied that it would get out the same way it got in, and when he had to spell out exactly what he meant by these words Doreen was horrified – so much so that immediately after the confinement she thrust the child from her with some words along the lines of "take it away! Take it away!"

Sadly, this led to Doreen having a nervous breakdown and made it difficult if not impossible for her to bond with her daughter. It was only in much later years that a working relationship was achieved.

Many young children go through the phase of having imaginary friends and playmates… Most of the time their parents smile indulgently and most of the time the child grows out of the phase as they have to start grappling with schools, homework, family dramas and the reality of life. More latterly things like X-Box and Play Station, mobile phones, faceBook and chat rooms soon make imaginary friends highly un-cool and laughably redundant. And yet, with Sandy things were very different.

From as early as she can remember she was always aware of "other people" around her. Initially she could hear their voices although it was not always clear what they were saying, and she could always sense their presence although she could not always see them. However, by the age of five or six she seems to have refined her talents; she was hearing words and conversations and clearly seeing faces of what she thought of as being her "other world" friends. For her this was a totally natural occurrence, something that became second nature that she regarded as being quite normal and therefore never questioned. In Sandy's own words, she was nearly always alone, but never lonely!

Her mother Doreen had a very different view, however, and she actively discouraged Sandy from making any reference to her spirit friends. She would frequently warn Sandy about the men in the yellow van, saying that they would "come to take her away" – and to be precise, to the mental asylum in Macclesfield. It is a matter of conjecture – was Doreen frightened for Sandy because of what was happening to her, or was she frightened *of* Sandy because of her increasingly powerful link with this "other" world that had become such an integral part of her life? Either way Doreen's discouragement graduated into a state of total forbiddance, perhaps because by then, Sandy had two younger sisters called Elaine and Angela with whom she shared a bedroom. Not entirely surprisingly these two girls would get very scared and hide under the blankets when Sandy would casually announce that the spirit people had arrived!

There is some beautiful irony in this insofar that over the years Elaine has developed into being a highly gifted medium in her own right with some very potent healing gifts, while Angela, who for most of her life has been quite "normal" has suddenly begun to experience the stirrings of latent clairvoyant ability!

Anyway, like many gone before her and no doubt like many who will come after, Sandy learned to be silent, to cover and hide her gift, to wrap it up and keep it secret from the world. By now she was in her early teens and there were other matters pressing.

It is worthwhile pausing at this point to analyse and assess the circumstances surrounding Sandy's extraordinary early childhood and to acknowledge that when the powers of clairvoyant perception are gifted to someone, that person is seldom of high born rank but more usually is someone from an ordinary working-class background. It is almost as though Spirit seeks a blank canvas with which to work, channelling through the mind and emotions of someone without intellectual pretensions or preconceptions and who can accept the presence of Spirit at face value. Furthermore, Spirit always seems to choose someone who has experienced a wee bit more than their fair share of human suffering. To be sure there are exceptions, but for every exception to the rule there are a dozen examples that adhere to it. And so it was with Sandy.

Therefore, I feel that Sandy's assessment of having had a "normal, happy childhood" must be questioned. Her very early years were spent in quite a degree of isolation. She lived with her parents in an old stone house set into a craggy hill side. This was "Cumberland House" and it was surrounded by a high stone wall, with a single point of entry and exit. Sandy thinks of her birth place as being somewhere "behind high walls" which gives some insight to her state of mind as a young child. She was constantly seeking approval and acceptance from a much loved but indifferent mother, the only consolation being her father's understanding and his efforts to compensate.

When she was seven years old her mother disappeared off the scene for the better part of two years, incarcerated in a local sanatorium with TB. In this modern day and age, the disease has virtually been eradicated (although recent figures show a worrying tendency that suggests it may be on the increase in certain areas) but back in the 1950s tuberculosis was a common ailment which not everyone survived. There were occasional visits to see her mother in the sanatorium, but they were few and far between.

From Sandy's point of view, no sooner had her mother got back home than her father was hauled off into hospital with a severe coronary condition: As a younger man, he had scarlet fever which had damaged his heart valves, and now those valves were weakening. In our 21st century, this would be a health condition that caused concern, but with the wonders of modern medical science, it would lead to some quite routine surgery, valve repair or replacement, and a few weeks in hospital recuperating. However, in the late 1950s this health condition was a death sentence.

Sandy remembers her father talking to her a little while before her 13th birthday, and trying to tell her that he was going to die. Sandy had absolutely no idea of this concept, what it meant or what her father's words implied.

Reuben Williamson died on October 11th 1960. Sandy recalls opening some cards and small presents on November 25th 1960 and then a few days later, there were more presents to be opened. When she asked her mother what these were for, Doreen told her that they were her birthday presents, and Sandy, somewhat puzzled, pointed out that whoever had sent them were a bit late because she'd just had her birthday, and Doreen with a rare flash of love and concern, had to point out that they were her 14th birthday presents, a year on from her father's death.

To this day Sandy has no memory or recall of that missing year between her 13th and 14th birthdays. It is a complete and total blank – which is a very interesting piece of information to the psychic investigator who might well ask where her mind and memories had gone in that critical missing year of adolescence. If Sandy wasn't "with us" in that year, where exactly was she and what relevance might that have to her later clairvoyant development?

Reading between the lines one gets the impression that there may have been an upsurge in the degree of psychic energy around Sandy at this time, but as far as Sandy was concerned, things just carried on as normal. She got into the habit of taking long walks across the peaks but seldom would this be without some form of spirit company. She has a clear memory of sitting in a summer meadow with a fellow walker, just talking about the weather and the loveliness of the day… A strand of meadowsweet fell upon her foot and she leaned forward to brush it off, and then turning, realized that she was quite alone in the field. Her companion, for all the world someone of corporeal flesh and blood, had simply disappeared. Some people might have been scared to death by this experience, but Sandy accepted it without question and without fear. After all, this was something that happened to her quite regularly.

She acknowledges that even at this young age she was acting as an involuntary medium and would frequently feel compelled to pass messages on to people, usually total strangers whom she'd never met before or since. One such occasion she remembers very well.

She was walking through the local park and in the distance, she saw two women approaching her, deep in conversation. With absolute clarity, she heard a voice in her ear saying "Hello, my name's Alan, and that lady coming towards you, the one on the left, that's my wife. Please *please* tell her that I'm safe and well, that I love her and want to thank her very much for what she did for me and please tell her to thank Robert for his support."

Having contact with spirit was one thing but passing such a personal message to a total stranger was another and as the two women drew closer and closer Sandy became more and more agitated upon the horns of her dilemma. She determined that she would say nothing but then at the last moment, as she was actually passing the two women, she heard Alan's voice begging her to convey the message.

So, in the end she turned around and confronted the lady on the left and said "Excuse me, I know you'll think I'm mad, but I've got a message for you from Alan. He wants you to know that he's safe and well, that he loves you very much, and he wants to thank you for what you did for him and he also wants to say thank you to Robert for his support..."

The lady burst into tears and Sandy beat a hasty retreat, but quite some time later Sandy learned that the woman's husband had been terminally ill with an extremely painful cancer. He had eventually slipped into a coma and after months of watching him suffer she finally found the courage to tell the doctors to turn off the life support system. This had only been six weeks earlier and she was feeling incredibly guilty and depressed about this until Sandy's casual words on a pathway in a park took away the guilt and gave her a new lease of life.

Sandy's early teens were tough years. She coped reasonably well at school and up until the death of her father would frequently get "A" grades for her work. Nevertheless, it was clear that she was no great academic and there was a constant shadow of poverty hanging like a cloud over her home life. With her mother and sister, she lived a very hand to mouth existence and by her own admission, her self-esteem was very low.

There was a change for the better when she was 14 and started going out with her first boyfriend. She met a young man called David who was five years her senior. He formally approached Doreen and asked permission to court Sandy, which Doreen gave, albeit with stringent conditions. This was 1961 and as anyone who grew up in the early 60s will confirm, in some respects it was a less restrictive era with far less suspicion and paranoia than is usually found in the so-called enlightened times of the present day.

When she was 16 Sandy and David became engaged but by the time she was 18 it was clear that the relationship wasn't going to work, so by mutual agreement and with a fair share of pain for both parties, they broke it off.

Sandy had left school at 15 without any qualifications, which was quite the norm back in those days when an education was perceived as a privilege rather than a divine right. Her first job had been as a seamstress for a lingerie company. She had a good eye for detail and was quite interested in fashion and design. After the break with David she started her second job, this time with the Bowater Scott paper company and here she met a charismatic fellow called Tony, falling head over heels in love with him almost instantly.

The cynic might say she bounced into Tony's arms on the rebound from the broken engagement and while there may be an element of truth in this, it is also true that Sandy was desperate for a home and a family of her own. She longed for stability and believed that Tony could provide the safety and security that had been missing from her life thus far.

And so, after a whirlwind romance and while still only 18, Sandy married Tony in 1966, giving birth to her first son Dale a year later in 1967 and her second son Adrian two years after that in 1969.

There is that well known old adage that says, "marry in haste, repent at leisure" which obviously Sandy had never heard. Perhaps both she and Tony had made the mistake that many couples make when starting out on a relationship – the woman thinking she will be able to change her man and the man thinking his woman will never change. One way or the other the marriage was not a success. To her credit, for the sake of her sons and in pursuit of the marital ideal of stability and security, Sandy stuck with the marriage for almost 10 years before she finally came to realize that the union was not working and never *could* work, no matter how much time and effort she put into it.

There can be no doubt that Sandy loved Tony very much but he proved impossible to live with. A working-class lad from the mill, he had absolutely no ambition or curiosity about life. His world revolved around the TV and a regular supply of newspapers and cigarettes from the shop at the bottom of a very steep hill down the road from where they lived. Hail rain or shine Sandy was expected to negotiate the hill in pursuit of her husband's simple pleasures – because that's what working class wives did in those days – and during her two pregnancies when the road was covered with ice Sandy would weep in frustration and the fear of falling as she struggled tentatively down to the shop and then back up to the house.

Tony did not socialize. He simply did not see the need. He had never learned to drive and refused to buy a car. If the local bus was good enough for his Mam and Dad it was good enough for him. Sandy, screaming with domestic claustrophobia, squirreled away a few pounds here and there and finally she passed her driving test and bought a small car – but it took quite a while for her to pluck up the courage to tell her husband that the car parked outside the house was, in fact, hers!

Sandy had married Tony in the hope of realising her dream of having a family of her own. Sadly, Tony wasn't in the least bit family orientated and it got to the point where she simply couldn't stand it anymore. The spirit world which had been present but passive throughout her 20s now began to agitate and become impatient for change. From Sandy's point of view there had to be more to life than her husband's newspapers and cigarettes, the racing on the television and that blasted hill. Spirit made her ever more curious to find out what was around the next corner of life, constantly encouraging her to break free from the unrewarding strangle hold of her present domestic situation.

After 10 years she finally admitted defeat. She felt pushed, partly by her own curiosity and ambition, but more so by Spirit, to move on... So, move on she did. This was in 1975 and it was a case of straight out of the frying pan into the fire!

Two: Rolling Dice

Determined to make a brand new start, Sandy rented a large old house in New Mills and began training as a community nurse. She found this work engaging and rewarding not least because it brought her into contact with a whole host of new people and gave her the beginnings of a social life. After the claustrophobic isolation of her years with Tony this was a most welcome novelty. She wasn't looking for wild parties or any degree of unbridled hedonism but it was nice to be able to meet friends for coffee or the occasional drink. Just being able to get out a bit more than had been previously possible added some sparkle to this heady mix. It would be wrong to say that her personality changed overnight but within a relatively short period of time she became significantly more gregarious and relaxed.

Although it must sound like a contradiction this was only possible because she maintained a rigid code of self-discipline. In this new, independent life, she was in charge and in control and it was she who would decide what she did, when she did it and who she did it with. The years with Tony had inflicted many scars and she was determined not to travel that road again. As such, friendships were fine and a few dinner dates were acceptable, but there was no way – absolutely no way – she was going to commit herself to another relationship. When gentlemen suggested they might enjoy a whisky and sofa she always said, "no thanks, I'll have a gin and platonic." She had her job, her friends and her children and that was more than enough.

And then…

Sandy had an Uncle Alan. Only five years older than Sandy, they'd grown up more on a brother and sister basis than uncle and niece. Alan had a friend, a merchant navy officer called Michael and he was very eager that his friend and his niece should meet. Not exactly brimming over with enthusiasm, Sandy went along to join her uncle and his friend down at a local watering hole and it has to be said that she was not impressed by what she saw. To her eyes Michael Ingham seemed rather scruffy and casual; his clothes were excessively colourful and his hair, despite the era, was far too long. He may well have been a respectable engineer in the merchant navy but in Sandy's opinion he looked like a refugee who'd got lost on his way home from Woodstock.

Michael, on the other hand, was well pleased with what he saw and was keen to see more of Sandy. Alan, in response to his friend's reaction, kept on at Sandy to go out with Michael on a date and finally, just to shut her uncle up, she finally relented and agreed to go out on "just one date".

Much to her surprise Sandy quite enjoyed her evening out and that first date led to others. This was strictly a platonic friendship but Sandy's admiration for Michael steadily grew as she became increasingly aware of his sensitivity and intelligence. She had learned to her cost that good looks alone made a poor foundation stone upon which to build a relationship.

Michael's emotions and romantic ambitions obviously went a lot deeper, so much so that in March of 1976 he asked Sandy to marry him – which was a proposal that Sandy promptly turned down. Not wanting to cause unnecessary hurt, she felt duty bound to explain her reasons, making it clear that if she were ever to marry again it would be to someone who valued the family ideal, and therefore if Mike wanted her then he would have to give up the navy, stop drinking quite so much and generally tidy up his act across the board. He was about to embark on a tour of duty and Sandy told him to spend the next few months at sea thinking about things and making sure that he was clear in his own mind about what he really wanted.

While some men might have told Sandy where to put her

precious family ideal, Michael Ingham was made of sterner stuff. He was patient and persistent and had bonded with Sandy's two sons, Dale and Adrian, making it quite clear that he was more than capable of filling the incredibly difficult step-father role. Also, it has to be said that sometimes absence does make the heart grow fonder and either way Sandy finally changed her mind and said yes – and she became Michael's wife at the end of 1976.

They say "be careful what you wish for in case your wish comes true". Sandy had always wished for a secure family life and now, to all intents and purposes, she had it. Steady job, regular income, doting husband and two fine sons. In every way they were also Michael's sons – but Michael wanted a child of his own.

This put Sandy in a quandary. She'd always wanted two children, had planned on having two children and now she'd got her two children. The idea of having a third gave Sandy cause to ponder long and hard. Having a baby is no easy thing – which is something that all mothers know but no man can ever fully understand – but she finally came to realize that she could not deny Michael. He had given up much for the sake of the family ideal so was it not natural that he should now want to expand the family and establish a blood line of his own?

This decision led to the birth of Sandy's third child, this time a beautiful daughter whom they named Lee-Anne, and who arrived just in time for Christmas on December 23rd 1977.

During the early years of her marriage to Michael, Sandy's friends in the spirit world became notably more active, although in the most subtle of ways. There were no shattering epiphanies or fingers of God splitting the heavens on the road to Damascus; there were no revelations of secret wisdom or amazing paranormal experiences that might make interesting reading in the red banner press or the Fortean Times. Rather, it was all very gentle and low key.

Putting it in context, Sandy had no formal knowledge of spiritualism and she knew nothing of the mechanics of clairvoyance. She had never been to a spiritualist church and indeed her view of religion was vague and ill-defined.

As an eight-year-old girl she had found herself strangely attracted to churches and had been an eager attendee of various Sunday schools. As a child, she went to church quite regularly, not out of any great conviction, but partly because it was the thing to do in Derbyshire's High Peak District and partly because she felt that her friends in the spirit world wanted her to look at the different orthodox religions and learn something about them.

By the time she got to 21 and had a few years' life experience behind her, it had become abundantly clear that the church had none of the answers she was looking for and couldn't offer any help. It slowly dawned on her that her own spiritual pathway was the right one – at least for her – and from that point onwards she became much more confident in her own faith and belief.

If you had asked her to verbalize her belief structure she would have struggled to comply because this was something she felt deep down inside and that she could not easily put into words. In fact, at that time in her life, it couldn't be put into words at all. But there was an interweaving of awareness within her, both natural and constant, that proclaimed the presence of another world filled with the spiritual identities of those people who had moved on from this life to the next and to Sandy this was a totally normal state of affairs. However, still influenced by the lessons of her childhood she remained silent and kept her secret knowledge to herself – although, as we shall see, circumstances conspired to make this increasingly difficult.

An early wakeup call came when it gradually became apparent that her younger son, Adrian, had some really quite remarkable healing gifts. Sandy would occasionally complain of a headache and Adrian, not yet three years old, would reach up to his mother's face with his chubby little hands, lay a baby's finger on her forehead and say, "Make better – make better" and within a short time the headache would subside.

One can ruminate on the possibilities of coincidence and psychosomatosis, but these incidents became quite frequent, even to the extent that when Sandy had a headache she would lift Adrian in her arms, point to her head and say, "Adrian make better" and as sure as God makes green apples in English orchards, Sandy's headache would disappear.

The romantic might wax lyrical about the psychic bonds between mother and son while the cynic and the sceptic might look at Sandy and accuse her of the delusional wish fulfilment that many mothers seem to have with their sons. That criticism, however, falls flat on its face when one considers Adrian's ability to heal a third party and not just of an elusive headache but of a visible ailment.

After Sandy had left home to marry Tony, her mother Doreen had never been heavily involved in her daughter's life and their meetings were rare and irregular. However on a weekend visit, when Adrian was about four, Doreen turned up with a number of very unpleasant and unsightly warts on one of her hands. To a curious little boy who had never seen a wart before this must have been a major event. When he tried to touch his grandmother's hand she pulled it away quickly, saying "No Adrian, poorly hand! Don't touch. Nasty!" To which, the little boy pointed at the hand and said "Poorly hand. Make better!" And 24 hours later, there wasn't a wart to be seen!

This story might sound incredible and the sceptics may throw up their hands in derision, but there are many such cases of healing taking place every day all over the world. They are well documented and in Sandy and Adrian's case there are independent witnesses.

Remembering how she was forced to suppress her natural talents in her own childhood, Sandy was quick to encourage Adrian and to create a safe environment for both her children in which they could blossom and bloom without fear or restriction. This seems to have paid dividends insofar as her children have flourished and not only is she loved as their mother, she is liked and respected as their friend. This is something that every mother assumes she will inherit as some form of divine right, but 19 out of 20 ends up being bitterly disappointed. As the odd one out of 20, Sandy considers herself most fortunate.

As a footnote, it is most reassuring to know that Adrian has never lost his healing gifts and they have matured and strengthened over the years. He has never broadcast or publicized his talents and has always worked quietly and discreetly in the background to bring succour and comfort to those in need, and especially to his close friends and colleagues. This latter point is especially relevant, considering Adrian's job. He's a career soldier specialising in bomb disposal!

Another way in which Spirit made its presence felt was in bringing people to Sandy who needed help and reassurance. She would frequently be approached by total strangers, be drawn into conversation with them, then find herself listening to their life stories. During the conversation Sandy would be touched by a spiritual presence, inevitably someone connected to the person she was with, who would tell Sandy things that she would pass on. For example, a woman was once talking to her about her recently deceased brother and Sandy immediately thought "Oh yes, that was Jeremy and he died on his motor bike…"

Initially Sandy maintained the discipline of silence, but occasionally things would slip out quite inadvertently. When it became increasingly obvious that the people she was with welcomed anything she said that could provide evidence that their loved ones were still around, she gradually became a bit more relaxed about the process – but even then, she never went looking for such contacts and never announced or publicized her abilities of mediumship. If she found herself doing ad hoc readings for people then this was fine. It was not for profit or financial gain, but simply to bring some reassurance that their loved ones, although passed over, were alive and well on the other side.

Her husband, Mike, seems to have taken this in his stride. Sandy did not tell him about her spirit world connection and he was often puzzled and bemused by his wife's popularity with total strangers. Then something happened that alerted him to the fact that the woman he'd married wasn't just your average girl next door.

They had been watching television one night and had stayed up quite late to watch a programme about Uri Geller, the Israeli mentalist who came to public prominence in the late 70s by bending spoons and other metallic objects. Mike commented that it was all a bit unbelievable and postulated the idea that Geller was just a clever stage magician. He was surprised by Sandy's reaction. She defended Geller, saying that all things had energy, especially metal, and this was something that she herself could tap into.

Mike didn't say anything, but on their way to the bedroom he picked up a dice that had been laying loose on the children's snakes and ladders game and concealed it in his fist.

"Right Sandy," he said, as they entered the bedroom. "Tell me what I'm holding in my hand!"

"Oh that's easy enough," she laughed back at him. "You're holding a dice!"

Mike was impressed, but decided to take it to the next level. He rolled the dice in his palm, keeping the face covered by his other hand.

"Okay, what number is showing if I take my hand away?"

Sandy thought about it for less than a second. "Number five," she said – and sure enough, when Mike removed his hand the dice was showing the number five.

When questioned about it afterwards Mike says he wasn't surprised to discover that his wife had these unusual abilities. She didn't make a big thing of them, and so neither did he. Having said that, he would occasionally set her little tests… She always passed them with flying colours until one day she got fed up and told him she wasn't going to play any more games and that he'd just have to accept her as she was. Again, this was no problem for Mike, for it was something he'd already done.

In 1981 Sandy began to get that restless feeling, the same feeling she'd had in her last days with Tony, that said it was time to move on… Time for a change. This coincided with a burgeoning desire within Mike to launch his own marine engineering business. They decided to get out of Derbyshire and because property was cheaper over in Lincolnshire they bought a house in a small village close to Lincoln. Sandy knew she'd been manoeuvred into this new location by Spirit. She didn't know why, but she was destined to find out very quickly.

Three: Bridlington 2011

One day, quite early in the process of writing this book, I drove over to Sandy's home in Bridlington to conduct an information gathering interview, which is an essential aspect of writing a biography when the subject of the biography is still alive and kicking! Although she had been totally open and forthcoming about her life thus far, there was one area that I wanted to explore in much greater depth, namely the mechanics and details of her contact with the spirit world.

Committed spiritualists may understand the concept of receiving messages from, or being "pushed" and "influenced" by Spirit but to the man in the street this is just so much mystical gobbledegook. When my brother-in-law or my nephew start talking to me about computers and IT then I have exactly the same problem. To clarify this in lay terms I needed Sandy to spell it out with all the I's dotted and the T's crossed. What is it actually like to be touched by a supernatural force and what is it actually like to be involved in a conversation with someone who has died?

It is in our human nature to be fearful of things we don't understand and to be suspicious of those things that scare us or are alien to us in any way. We are all Xenophobes at heart with the roots of our fear echoing back to our tribal days of living in caves: what made that weird scraping noise in the dead of the night? What stalks us in the dark that wasn't there when it was light?

In the 20th and 21st centuries these superstitions have been fuelled by a plethora of ghost stories, horror novels and scary movies etc, that by and large present the supernatural as something to be frightened of. Science does not help by insisting that all things must have a logical explanation before they can be accepted as a matter of fact and the Christian church, as a body politic, has added fuel to the flames by stating categorically and quite arrogantly that the only way to God is through Jesus Christ.

On top of all this we have a host of other "fears" drummed into us by media and the state – the fear of unemployment, mugging, being knifed or burgled, the fear of the falling pound and the rising tide of HIV, the fear of first this conspiracy and then the next, the fear of not being able to keep up the repayments on the mortgage, never mind keeping up with the Joneses... The fear of being damned if we do not conform to the church's view of religion and damned by the state if we do not conform to their idea of what our role should be in their society! We become increasingly scared of death and because we are being conditioned to be scared of everything, we are even becoming scared of life! In short, we are living within a permanent veil of fear and although much of it is subliminal, it still exercises an effect upon our consciousness. For many people, it is simply a bridge too far to ask them to believe in the possibility of communicating with the dead.

They may be happy to believe in God in general terms and they may accept the concept of spirituality in an amorphous sense; they might like to believe in heaven and an afterlife, but present them with the shade of their Auntie Annie who got knocked over by a bus outside the Sheffield Co-op in 1974 and most would flee screaming.

Sandy, like all spiritualists, works hard to remove the fear of death by offering evidence for life after death, but for this to be effective the evidence needs to be pretty conclusive and stand up to investigation – and that's what took me to Bridlington that sunny Saturday in July.

Sandy's home is a light and airy place, clean, tidy and well ordered. There are no creepy cobwebs or piles of old books, no lurking shadows, no sign of any crystal balls or well-thumbed packs of Tarot cards. As she took me through into the sitting room and Mike went off to make some coffee, the only alien presence was the occasional squawk from a hyperactive cockatiel.

Once we'd got through the usual pleasantries I started the interview by asking Sandy to give me a specific example of how her life had been affected by spiritual intervention – something other than just being "pushed" or "influenced" – that provided *her* with absolute proof that the spirit world was real and not just the figment of an over active imagination.

First of all, she looked uncomfortable, as though wrestling with an inner conflict. Then with a small smile and a "what the hell" shrug of her shoulders, she gave me the information I was looking for.

Back in the mid-1970s while still living with Tony in New Mills, Sandy arrived at the lowest ebb in her life. So much so that she decided to end it. You will no doubt appreciate that there was a lot more behind this decision, both in Sandy's childhood and her years with Tony, than we have revealed in the last two chapters. Suffice to say that this decision was not taken lightly and there were some quite understandable motives at its core. From what she told me I don't think that she particularly wanted to die, it was just that the pain of living was too much to bear. It was also clear from her words that this was not a histrionic or impulsive decision, rather one that she had arrived at over a period of time after careful thought and consideration.

Thankfully the vast majority of people never experience this nadir of the soul, but those who have been there will tell you that you don't just wake up one morning and say, "I'm not very happy so I'm going to kill myself today" – rather it is usually as the result of going through a long period of suffering, sometimes of desperation and frequently a goodly portion of both, wherein the pain of living outweighs the fear of dying and death is seen as the only solution.

In the Judo-Christian culture of the Western world, no doubt based upon the dictate of the church, suicide is perceived to be a sin and indeed, ridiculous as it might sound, in British law it is a criminal offense. However, in many other cultures the taking of one's own life is regarded as a most noble exit from this world and one only has to look at the Jihadis of Islam or the Kamikaze tradition of Japan to find obvious examples.

I don't suppose Sandy gave these finer philosophical points a moment's thought. As far as she was concerned she'd had enough and she was leaving. Making very sure she was not going to be found before the deed was done, she locked all the doors and windows then took a very large dose of Paracetamol and Anadin washed down with liberal quantities of wine. She made herself comfortable in an armchair and before very long started feeling very woozy and distant. There was no doubt in Sandy's mind that she was dying.

Through the haze she gradually became aware of the front door bell ringing insistently. As the ringing turned into an aggressive banging she dragged herself out of the chair to see what all the fuss was about, too deeply affected by the drugs and the alcohol to remember what she had done. Much to her surprise she found her Uncle Alan at the door... which is where this story starts getting very interesting.

Although related, and despite the fact that Alan had been incredibly supportive in loco parentis when her father had died, they really didn't see very much of each other at this time. If there were a couple of casual meetings in any given year, that was about it. Alan had been driving home from work, had actually passed Sandy's house and was another 10 miles down the road before he'd suddenly felt compelled to stop and turn the car around and drive back the 10 miles he'd just travelled. Something was telling him that he absolutely *had* to go and see Sandy.

And when he *did* finally see her he immediately knew that something was very wrong.

"Good God, Sandy, you look absolutely awful," he said, entering the house even though Sandy was none too pleased to see him. "What on earth's wrong?"

"I'm not feeling very well," Sandy slurred stubbornly, "and I'm sorry, but this isn't a good time for a visit."

Alan wasn't having any of this and immediately called an ambulance… and on the way to the hospital Sandy's spirit left her body and she knew she was dying. She looked down at her prostrate body from the roof of the vehicle, remembers seeing Alan sitting next to her with his head in his hands, and then there was simply a feeling of drifting away into the sweet nothingness of oblivion.

To her very great surprise she regained consciousness in a hospital bed, feeling completely detached and totally disoriented. There was a nurse by her bedside and Sandy feebly asked her where the man was who'd told her where she had come to and where she had to go. Needless to say, the nurse was baffled and put Sandy's words down to wild ramblings, but as far as Sandy was concerned she had woken in the bed with a strong male presence just behind her. She never saw his body, but even after all these years she remembers his voice clearly – a rich velvety voice that reminded her of Cliff Richard and liquid chocolate. In that state somewhere between sleep and wakefulness the voice had spoken to her quite clearly. "It's not your time yet Sandy and you've got to go back."

Sandy is very aware of two things. First of all, if something hadn't made her Uncle Alan stop in his tracks and then direct him back to her front door, Sandy would have died that day back in 1974. Secondly, she had stood on the doorstep of death by the gates of heaven and to this day cannot understand why she didn't have a good look around while she was there.

This experience was a major turning point in Sandy's life and it opened the door to a greater degree of spiritual potency. It seems that coming so close to death rekindled some fresh hope and faith in life and she knew that if she had been sent back because it wasn't her time to go, then there had to be a reason for it. Not just a reason but a purpose.

The next question on my agenda was a very important one. I needed to explore the methodology of Sandy's communication with the spirit world and I asked her to describe the experience.

"Well," she said briskly, "I'm not a clairaudient so I don't hear words spoken in my ear. I'm *clairsentient* and that means I get the words and messages projected directly into my head. I always know when a spirit is moving in close to me because I get this icy cold shiver immediately followed by a beautiful sensation of warmth. It's all about a joining of energies and it feels as though there's an electric current crackling all around me..."

There is a lovely little demonstration that any two people can do which in a small way illustrates this merging of energies. If person number one closes their eyes and person number two brings their hand two or three inches (sometimes centimetres, depending on the subjects) in front of their face, or over their head or even over their hand, then person number one will frequently feel this presence as person number two's hand penetrates the human etheric field – but at no time makes physical contact with the body. Try it and prove the point for yourself.

Next, I asked Sandy about spirit guides.

"We all have them," she chuckled, "although it's true to say that most people don't know that they've got one. I call these guides the *Door Keepers*. They're with us every step of the way through life and they act as our link between this world and the next. They help us on our way and try to keep us out of trouble. Some people might call them our guardian angels while more sceptical folk might just think of them as being our instinct and intuition. Either way you can be driving fast along a road and find yourself slowing down for no apparent reason – just before a speed camera flashes or a kiddie runs off the pavement. You can be all set to get on a train or a plane and then something tells you not to do it… Catch another train or take another flight, and when the train crashes or the plane comes down in the middle of the ocean, then you know why you've been warned!

"For me it works in other ways as well. I remember a good few years ago now when those two little girls from Soham had gone missing and they were interviewing Ian Huntley on the television and he was going on about how much he hoped they would be found and how he was doing everything to help the police… I knew straight away that he'd done it. Absolutely without any shadow of a doubt!

"My Door Keeper guide is a white South African who'd have been alive a couple of hundred years ago. He would either have been a doctor or, if not a doctor, some kind of healer or herbalist. When I asked him to give me his name it was fairly unpronounceable so I've always called him Baal because that's about the closest I can get. I've done a bit of research into the name and have discovered that it's a Semitic word with very complex origins that basically means 'lord' or 'master'. I know that the name has some fairly negative connotations in the Christian world, after all, it's the name of a pagan god, but when I asked some Dutch friends of mine about it, they told me that Baal was quite a common name in Holland, a bit like Smith or Jones over here. Whenever I see him he has always got his back to me or his head is out of vision; I've repeatedly asked him to show me his face but he never has. At least that was true right up to the point of this book being written when Baal finally allowed his portrait to be drawn.

"My other principle guide is a North American Indian. I've no idea what he's called but I always have an impression of a white feather when he comes to me. Now don't get me wrong, I am not going to be so corny or clichéd as to call this guy White Feather. I don't know what his name is and all I'm doing is telling you what I see when he makes his presence felt.

"The vision of this guide is always the same. First of all, I see the leg and fetlocks of a big chestnut coloured horse then my eyes travel up until I see the Indian's legs, then his thighs, then his torso and finally his face. He really is a magnificent fellow, brimming with health and vitality. When either of my guides is giving me a message it comes through as a thought form, and sometimes if they are there together it's hard to work out which message is coming from whom. When I see my guides, their images are always tinged with beautiful black and gold auras. I don't know if those colours are significant or anything, but they really are quite spectacular.

"I have another guide who is an extremely beautiful young woman with the most amazing eyes. Until a few weeks ago I didn't know her name but she always brings through people who have only very recently passed over. In a way, this is a bit strange because I sense that she herself has been in spirit for many years. I got into the habit of calling her my Unknown Lady. At least, she was unknown to me, other than as a guide, but I was positive that someone out there would look at her picture and know exactly who she was.

"Then only the other week, something really strange happened. I was contacted by a gentleman in Australia, a retired airline pilot who also happened to be a spiritualist, who wanted me to do a picture for his daughter. I asked him if he'd seen any of my work and he told me no, and that he'd only picked up my name from the internet. On impulse, I sent him a portrait of the Unknown Lady and it just about blew his socks off. He had three daughters, two living called Samantha and Elaine, and one who had passed over called Angela. My picture was the spitting image of his late daughter Angela! So, in a very roundabout way, this was another mystery solved, and as with Baal's portrait, I think I want to put it down to the creation of this book. It seems to have stirred up a few psychic waves and vibrations.

"I've got one other guide and he made his presence felt only relatively recently when I started doing the drawings. He is clearly identified as someone I call Leo and when I'm doing the sketching it is definitely him who's pushing the pencil around in my hands. I sense that Leo is a very old spirit and has been passed over for several hundred years. Instinct tells me he might have been Italian around the time of the renaissance, but that's just my gut feeling and I can't back it up with anything…"

Sandy continues – "When I'm actually sitting with some-body doing a reading a spirit will sometimes come in and stand or sit next to me and they are totally real. There are no ghostly vapours or transparent apparitions, but just the same as if they were there in the flesh. I've never been able to work out why it's like this for some people but not for others. The only thing I do know is that unlike some other mediums my doorways never close and I'm always wide open for spirit to come in and use me whenever they need to. People ask me what it's like to see a spirit and this is so hard to describe – but look at this…" Sandy pulled out a very strange piece of artwork which, quite frankly, didn't look like anything much at all other than a sophisticated ink blot. "Just look at this image really hard for a minute, really study it, and then shut your eyes tightly – and the after image you get is a bit like the spirit people I see when I'm receiving a message or doing a drawing for someone."

Stare at the image for a few minutes and then close your eyes. The image left on the retina of the eye gives you an idea of how Sandy sees spirits.

"I was in Marks and Spencer the other day, having a moan to the salesgirl about needing something to wear for my work on stage and when she asked me what I did I told her that I was a medium…

"She said that was very interesting and asked me who I tended to get… Well, ever since I went up to the counter I'd had this elderly gentleman with me in spirit. He was, he said, her Grandfather, and he told me that his name was Jeff. He was waving a big greeting card in his hand which I took to be a birthday card. So anyway, in answer to the salesgirl's question I said, "Oh anybody really, even someone's Granddad who might be called Jeff." Well, as you can imagine, that got her attention and we started talking and I told her that her Grandfather was wanting to wish someone a happy birthday. This puzzled her because no one she knew of had a birthday remotely close to this particular day and then she suddenly realized that the following day was her wedding anniversary!"

More recently Sandy was sitting for a photo shoot and as the photographer was snapping away merrily, Sandy was sketching as usual, and came up with the most amazing picture of the photographer's father. The photographer was amazed and Sandy was content with this extra little snippet of evidence.

Anyway, we'll pick up on the technical bits a little later on but for now it's time we got back to the narrative and we need to pick up the story at the point where Sandy and her family moved from New Mills to Lincoln.

The lady, now identified as "Angela," is responsible for bringing through messages from people who have only recently passed over.

Baal – South African Doctor, circa 1800

Leo, the 16ᵗʰ century guide directs the pencil in Sandy's hands

Four: Lincoln

So, late in 1981 Sandy and her family arrived in the tiny two street village of Little Sokum. It was picturesque, but very small – literally two straggling rows of houses that straddled a quiet stretch of the River Slea. Sandy's new home was a very modest bungalow right at the edge of the village, but to compensate for the size of the house the garden was quite enormous with the river running across the boundary.

They'd been there for a few days, busy with the business of unpacking and settling in and then they received their first visitor. Rather an unlikely welcoming committee in the form of a tousled-haired boy on a bike. He was about 13 years old and introduced himself as Dean. He said he hoped they'd be happy in their new home, talked about the local school at great length, and passed on some useful information about the local bus service into Lincoln (one bus a day, two on Saturday, and nothing on Sunday).

As he rode off on his wobbly two wheels Sandy felt impressed and reassured. If Little Sokum produced young boys like Dean then she felt she had no reason to fear for the welfare of her own children.

Coming to grips with a new home can be a bit of a nightmare; one lives amid a clutter of boxes, packing cases, displaced kitchen utensils, unplugged white goods and upended furniture and Sandy had her hands full – so much so that she really didn't give Dean another thought until some weeks later when she started feeling the boy's presence on a psychic level. Over the following few days he kept slipping in and out of her mind – she had never experienced anything quite like this before and found the whole experience puzzling and unsettling.

Then to her dismay and distress she found out that Dean had been shot in the head in a shooting accident – a 10 year old neighbour playing with his Dad's loaded shot gun – and that he was on a life support machine over at Lincoln District Hospital. He was in a deep coma and was not expected to live.

One cannot imagine the anguish and the agony of the boy's parents, especially when they came unwillingly to the decision to follow the doctor's advice and allowed the life support machine to be turned off. Dean's coma deepened and he finally passed away without regaining consciousness.

The only small up-side of this tragic event was now that he was in spirit, he was able to visit Sandy and make proper contact. He desperately wanted to talk to his mother, but Sandy had to tell him that she didn't know who his mother was or where she lived, although she went on to say that "If you can get her to come to me I'll be able to talk to her for you."

A couple of days later there was a tentative knock on Sandy's front door. Sandy opened up to find herself confronted by an attractive lady in her late 30s; attractive but tragic. It was clear that the woman had been crying and she was surrounded by an aura of great sorrow.

"Er, my name's Mary," the woman stammered, "and I know it sounds stupid, but I've got no idea what I'm doing here…"

"It's all right, my darling," Sandy said kindly. "I know exactly who you are and I've been expecting you, so come on in and I'll make you a cup of tea and we can have a chat."

This invitation led to a long conversation between Sandy and Dean's mother. Sandy told Mary all about the spirit world and Dean came through with a number of evidential messages to prove his post mortem survival. He brought love and reassurance, and as you might expect, Mary was over the moon. Knowing that her son was still alive, albeit in another dimension and that he was still with her in spirit, could not take away the feeling of loss but it did do a great deal to remove the desolation of bereavement.

Thoroughly delighted by what had transpired she rushed home to tell her husband John her good news.

Bad move.

I don't know what it is about some men, and when I say "some men" I suppose I mean most men, but they seem to be totally closed off from any degree of psychic sensitivity and hostile to the thought that there might just be something going on around them that they can't see, feel or touch for themselves. I've often wondered if it's beer, pubs, cars, sexual conquests and football that gets in the way of a man's ability to accept the spiritual and paranormal or whether it's because he's too damned scared or too damned stupid.

There are many exceptions to the rule and I could give you a list of scores of men that I have known or have heard of over the years who are some of the most sensitive and spiritual souls abroad on this azure planet of ours. You could start with the Dalai Lama and end up with people like Mike Ingham and Stephen Holbrook – but I suspect that for every Michael Ingham or Steve Holbrook there are hundreds of thousands of men who would reject the concept of a spiritual afterlife and a good percentage of those would even say that it was evil to even consider the possibility. What is wrong with these men? Do they have an agenda alien to the rest of us or are they so arrogant that they presume that anyone who disagrees with them must be mad, imprisoned, or burned at the stake?

With women there is an inverse proportion of acceptance and while a few females might vehemently deny the possibility of post mortem survival, the vast majority of the female sex has a more highly tuned degree of sensitivity and intuition which enables them to more readily grasp the concept. Is it that women are *not* into beer, pubs, cars, sexual conquest and football or is it because they are more in tune with nature and the natural vibrations of the planet? It is, I think, six of one and a couple of dozen of the other. Certainly the feminine role of motherhood has much to do with this.

Either way, Dean's mother rushed home to tell her husband John of the wonderful thing that had happened with Sandy and all she got for her trouble was condemnation, criticism and a verbal tirade of anger. In short, John was furious and forbade his wife ever to see Sandy again.

I have to say I have heard a score of different versions of this story over the years so John's reaction comes as no great surprise to me. It did come as a surprise to Mary though. She thought that her husband would be as pleased as she was to learn that Dean was all right, and his anger and overbearing attitude generated some anger within her own breast. As far as she was concerned, if Sandy Ingham could facilitate communication between her and her son, she was determined to carry on seeing Sandy, and if her husband didn't like it he could lump it.

So, she carried on visiting Sandy quite regularly – and John didn't like it at all, becoming more and more antagonistic and increasingly angry, with that anger not only directed towards his wife but towards Sandy as well.

In the end Sandy felt she had to speak directly to Dean. She told him that the situation was getting very difficult, that his father was angry enough to start causing some real problems and that both she and his mother, while determined to carry on with their quest, were actually becoming very concerned.

"There's only one thing that might defuse this situation," Sandy said at last. "Dean, my darling, you're going to have to give your dad proof that you're still around."

Dean agreed and he went about it in two ways; one quite subtle, the other full in the face.

First of all, he told his mother to let his father know that he had been with him when he was working in one of the fields. It had been a very hot day and John had been sweating profusely. He'd been wearing a bright multi-coloured sweater that Mary had knitted for him out of old remnants, and finally, in the middle of the field, out of view from anyone, John had stopped the tractor, taken off the jumper, and because it was of some special sentimental value, had folded it carefully beneath his seat.

Whatever John thought when Mary passed on this information to him, he knew with absolute certainty that no one could have seen him in the middle of the field. It was a very big field and John had a very small tractor.

Very shortly after that John opened his back kitchen door and clearly saw Dean waving to him from the bottom of the garden. Dean was full of smiles and gave his father the thumbs up sign before fading from view. There had been a world of distance between father and son but with that distance suddenly reduced to a few yards, if only for the duration of 10 or 12 seconds, John's attitude suddenly began to soften. He had been hostile and suspicious, but now he became very curious… And thankfully curious enough to listen to some of the things that Mary and Sandy were saying to him.

Much as Mike had done in the early days of their marriage, John felt compelled to set Sandy the usual "tests" to prove that she was for real. On one occasion he asked Sandy to tell him what he was holding in his hand, and initially Sandy struggled. John was actually holding one of the trial examples of the new £2 coin. They were few and far between and Sandy had never even heard of them let alone seen one. When her spirit guide told her that John was holding "a two-pound-coin" Sandy had to ask her guide to run that past her again to make sure she'd heard correctly. The message was repeated, so taking a leap of faith Sandy relayed it exactly as she'd heard it – and of course, she was quite right!

On another occasion while they were enjoying a drink in the beer garden of a local pub, John asked Sandy to tell him how long the present landlord had held tenure. Sandy came back immediately with the number 54 but wasn't sure if that meant the answer was 54 years or that the present landlord had taken over the pub in 1954. In this case it was the 54 years that won the prize.

But it was another incident that finally put the nail in the lid of John's scepticism. Mary had been swimming one morning and she'd called in for a cup of tea with Sandy on her way home. Dean made his presence felt and through Sandy, told his mother that she'd been swimming and that he'd been there with them, joining in the fun.

Mary had sighed. "I'd love to believe that's true," she'd said wistfully.

"It's perfectly true," Dean had replied "and I can prove it. When you get home, go into my old bedroom and look in the middle drawer of the chest of drawers and see what you find!"

Mary hurried back to her own house and went up to her son's bedroom. John and Mary had left it pretty well intact after his passing; certainly they'd tidied up and kept the room clean but basically all Dean's shoes and clothes were as he'd left them.

Rather tentatively she edged the middle drawer open and there among a pile of shirts and socks were Dean's swimming trunks and a big fluffy towel. Both the bathing suit and the towel were decidedly damp and smelt very faintly of chlorine…

John didn't exactly have an epiphany on his road to Damascus but gradually over the weeks and months – and then the years – he became one of Sandy's greatest friends and supporters. So much so that when Sandy finally got around to setting up a small development circle for spiritual awareness Mary became a founder member with John's full support. That was back in 1981 and although Sandy left when it was time to leave, the circle carried on for the following 30 years, finally coming to a natural conclusion in 2010. No small achievement!

Travelling along the pathway of her spiritual development Sandy had always followed a very solitary road but now in the early 80s she felt a need to formalize her knowledge and to reach out and make contact with other people who thought and felt as she did. This led to her visiting the spiritualist church over in the nearby town of Sleaford where she was welcomed with warmth and enthusiasm. It is quite remarkable that despite her history and experience, this was her very first visit to a spiritualist church, and in choosing Sleaford she was very lucky insofar as it was cheerful and modern with a young congregation. Even now there are still too many churches located in gloomy little rooms, rampant with dry rot and pitted with flaking plaster that offer safe haven to a dozen damp bodies on a cold winter's night as an elderly congregation gathers in the rather forlorn hope of a message from the world of spirit. Despite what some people might say, based on my own experience, it is very difficult to lift one's spiritual vibration when your feet are freezing cold and the atmosphere is redolent with the smell of last week's curry from the Indian restaurant next door.

Sandy felt very safe and comfortable at Sleaford. It was a calm and peaceful environment and was she was quickly invited to sit in the church's own development circle. It was while sitting in this circle one day that she picked up the very strong presence of a young girl who very much wanted to talk to her mother, but when she asked around the circle if anyone had a female child in spirit all the answers came back negative. The girl's presence persisted and so Sandy asked again if anyone had a female child in spirit and again the answer came back "no". Tuning in to the thought form language she always used when communicating with the spirit world she had to tell the young girl that she was sorry but she couldn't place the message – at which point the girl laughed merrily and said "What's the matter Mum? Can't you recognise your own daughter?"

This came as no small shock to Sandy for back in 1972 she'd had a miscarriage and hadn't even known that she was pregnant until she'd lost the baby! Her loss was part of a curious spate of passings... First of all her Grandfather died and then six weeks later, her Grandmother also passed over. Six weeks after that a nephew died, and six weeks after that Sandy had to deal with the miscarriage.

This incident with the lost baby prompted me to ask Sandy about this, because one of the questions mediums get asked most often is what happens to babies who die in the womb – and maybe the second most frequently asked question relates to cot deaths and babies who die while very young for no apparent reason. Sandy provided a detailed and informative answer.

"Before we are born, when we are still in spirit, we may well decide to live another life and if that happens we effectively come back to school for another lifetime's worth of lessons and experiences. We choose the parents that we're going to have, we choose the experiences that we need to experience in this lifetime and so we go from A to B to C to D. Our free will takes us from A to B... we may go in a straight line or we're more likely to deviate along different paths on the way as we become aware of different lessons we need to learn to help us progress and evolve on our spiritual pathway. This happens on a spiritual and subconscious level – in our earth plane bodies we probably don't have a clue as to what's going on.

"The spirit chooses its parents and the parents create the baby and all the time, the spirit is there watching the growth of the body that it will inhabit. Spirit is with that body every step of the way as it grows within the womb. Now, some people will say that the spirit doesn't enter the body until it's born, others will say from the very first cell division the spirit is within the baby's body. I'm not certain about the definitive answer to this and on one level I'm not sure that it matters very much. What does matter is that Spirit inspires the baby to be created and watches over it and Spirit is there whilst the host body is being built. One thing's for sure, and that is when the baby arrives red faced and yelling its little head off, Spirit and body are united as one."

At this point I interjected and asked her to explain what happens when the baby doesn't make it… If, for example, there is a miscarriage or a termination?

"It's still an experience that the spirit has had," Sandy answered. "Everything we do in our life is a learning curve."

"It may be a learning curve for the spirit, but at what cost to the parents?" I cut in.

"And thereby lies *their* learning curve and their experiences and what they chose to experience before they were born. The other thing to remember is that the baby, lost to them in the flesh, has, through this experience, forged a close spiritual bond with both its parents. That baby will be there with them, guiding and supporting them, for the rest of their days, still a member of that family, but there in spirit rather than being with them on the earth plane."

"So what you're saying," I said carefully, "is that all of our lives are interconnected, both in the flesh and in spirit?"

"Yes, of course. Absolutely," she confirmed. "When we're born there's a whole team of spirit friends and guides that help us along our pathway. I believe also (and have been told by spirit) that along the way there will be one or two 'opt out' positions throughout our lifetimes to go back… you know, the opportunity to go back home. I consider the spirit world as home. If you're lucky enough to go through your life having a fabulous time, well indeed how lucky you are, but the fact is life can be very dark and cruel… I've asked spirit about this because I want answers, I need to know. If we're supposed to learn from spirit then we have to ask questions about everything.

"For instance, look at this beautiful place we're in now…" Sandy gazed lovingly out of the French windows of her sitting room and surveyed her long fecund garden with a look of satisfaction and pleasure… "I've got birds out there by the thousand and they visit me because I feed them and I passionately adore them, and then there are the trees that I'm looking at through my window, the fluffy white clouds, the gorgeous blue sky. I just love this planet, I love life, every bit of life. Then, as you look deeper and deeper and more intensely into this life, oh my God it can be so ugly and evil… Not the planet but what we do with it. It doesn't end with us humans because cats will decimate the bird population – for fun? The fox will go into a hen house and destroy all the hens – what the hell for? Where's the pattern there? There is no pattern! It's not Godly and it's not good and I want to know why. What's gone wrong here? You could say it's the nature of life, but I'm sure than someone somewhere has got it wrong."

She was crackling with passion and righteous indignation and now that she was in her stride there was no stopping her. "Just look at all the wars going on around the world. This is a fine example of man's inhumanity to man. Spirit has got nothing to do with this and neither has God. Maybe it's a dirty trick of nature designed to keep the numbers down but as far as I can see, it's just an act of men."

"What about tsunamis and floods and earthquakes and all kinds of natural disasters?" I asked. "I mean, you can't really describe them as acts of Man so are they acts of God?"

"Well," she shrugged, "if you believe as I do that God is the power and energy of love and life, or even if you want to believe in the orthodox God as we're sold it, then no, I don't think they can be acts of God. We all get told that we should fear God, but why would we fear God? God is love and God is life. That's what it should be like but it doesn't always work. It isn't right and I believe that something has gone wrong with the whole philosophy, the whole creation process."

"Hang on," I said, trying to catch up "So, you'd agree that soldier killing soldier was an act of Man?"

"Yes."

"And that the tidal wave that kills 200,000 people in the Pacific is an act of nature but *not* an act of God?"

"Yes, it's a gross and excessive act of nature but I don't think it's an act of God. I don't believe in acts of God because I just believe that God is a universal energy. I believe it's the energy of love and light that we have in our lives; all that is good within us. If there is a Heaven and Hell then Heaven is living with God's love and Hell is living without it… It might sound like a cliché but God is love! That's my philosophy and we all have God in our hearts because we are all part of God in that way."

I pondered on that and thought I saw a couple of gaping holes in her philosophy. "What about some of the world's villains?" I asked. "I mean, for example, would you describe Adolf Hitler as a man who had love in his heart?"

"There's a capacity for good and evil in all of us," she answered. "Nothing is ever completely black and white. Sometimes, for whatever reason, as in Hitler's case, the balance is tipped. Adolf loved himself and he loved his Alsatian and Eva Braun. In his own way he loved his country. In some ways he was a brilliant man till he became a psychotic megalomaniac. But James, either way you look at it, love is love is love. We feel it as we give it and we feel it when we receive it, but it's not something that we can touch – it's only something that we can feel and different people will feel it in so many different ways. If you want it kept really simple, anything that makes you feel good, light, bright and happy is love. Anything that makes you feel the opposite of those things is the opposite of love."

Sandy paused thoughtfully and then changed the subject slightly. "I want answers to everything and my guides tell me things in story form. Once upon a time, many years ago now, I used to wear a cross and chain around my neck and one day I'd been chatting with my friends upstairs as I do every night, thanking them for the help they'd given me during the day, the communications that made people happy, and then as I was lying in bed I heard the voice of my guide asking me what I was wearing around my neck.

"I told him it was a crucifix and he asked me what I thought its purpose might be. I told him that it was a reminder that Jesus Christ had died on the cross to save the souls of all mankind.

"Oh, said the spirit, but surely this was an instrument of pain and torture, so why would you wear such a thing around your neck? I sort of repeated myself and said that I wore it so that I wouldn't forget that Jesus had died for us.

"My spirit guide said this was absolute rubbish – it was just something that had been told to me as a child – and then he asked me if I thought that Jesus wanted to die or did I think that he might just have been a young man who put an awful lot of effort into being educated in all the countries of the world that he travelled in – just because he expected to be killed?

"When it was put like that I had to agree that he wouldn't have gone through all of that if he'd expected to meet such a cruel end. Anyway the spirit seemed satisfied that I was getting to where I was supposed to go and he finally finished off his argument by pointing out that the symbol of the cross was given to all Christ's followers and they were told to keep it about their persons, lest they forget what happens to people who don't toe the line and follow the teaching of The Church. And that's why people wear crosses.

"Well, I've got to tell you mine was taken off my neck and

thrown as far as I could throw it. I won't have anything in the house, around my neck or anywhere near me that is an instrument of torture."

"This message, the one you've just told me about… This was a specific message from spirit?"

"Yes, it was absolutely."

"Can you identify the spirit?"

"Yes, as I've said, it was my principal guide, my South African healer."

I needed to pick her up on another point of major significance. "So, according to your guide, Jesus travelled to many different countries, but there's no reference to that in the bible."

"James, go read your bible. There's nothing in it at all about what Jesus did between being 12 and 30 years old and all I can tell you is that, according to my guide, he didn't just spend 18 years sunbathing on the beach by the Sea of Galilee!"

I had to concede that she had a point and her information coincides with a lot of independent research that you *won't* find in the Bible that suggests that Jesus did travel quite extensively throughout the known world of the time, visiting places as far flung as India and Britain. His uncle, Joseph of Arimathea was, after all, an international trader specialising in exotic spices and fine silks and it has often been mooted that Jesus travelled with him on many of his journeys. Another body of evidence indicates quite clearly that Jesus did have a number of different spiritual teachers during his short lifetime, notably the Essenes, and there is a volume of written, although obfuscated, evidence contained within the Dead Sea Scrolls that confirms that he was a member of that sect. Imagination encourages speculation and if Jesus did travel extensively with his Uncle, who is to say he did not study magic with the Druids of Britain or healing with the doctors and magicians of Egypt?

I could think of a hundred members of the clergy who

would pounce upon Sandy (and me) at this point like a clouder of cats going after a lame canary. In olden days gone by they would scream heresy and blasphemy, claim that Sandy had converse with a demon or an evil spirit and they'd have her burned at the stake as a witch before tea time. But this is the 21st century and in these more enlightened times, things have changed a bit, right?

All right, maybe a bit – but sadly, not nearly as much as you might think and there is still a hard core of very influential people in high and secret places who are ruthlessly determined to crush and suppress any thought or doctrine that does not coincide with their own… They see it as their inalienable right to govern, rule and control – and we'll talk more about them later.

Five: Bridlington Harbour and other Special Places

During the course of my life I have travelled extensively around the world and have enjoyed living and working in a number of different countries. On two occasions I have (or so I believed at the time) sold up and quit Britain for good in favour of other places that have had more to offer than the land of my birth. It is no secret that I don't like Britain very much… I hate the weather, loathe the politics and despair of our culture, our values and our social priorities. Those things about Britain that I *do* love, our language, history and traditions, have now become so contaminated and corrupted that I have long felt like Robert Heinlein's stranger in a strange land. And yet despite all my efforts to break free from British restraint I always seem to be dragged back to this country and inevitably, although I would much prefer to be in Cornwall, Dorset or Suffolk, I find myself struggling to survive in the North of England.

Why is this? What is this power, so much stronger than my own choice and free will, that keeps pulling me back and holding me in this place? I think that Sandy might have an answer – or at least part of an answer – to this question when she says that we end up being where Spirit wants us to be. Sometimes, if we are happy with the plan Spirit has for us, all is well, and sometimes if we are not, we can rail against it as much as we like but we are not going to be able to change anything until we have fulfilled the purpose that has been laid down by Spirit – and agreed by us at that time before our physical birth!

I know so many people who in the course of their lives never move very far from the place they were born and I know quite a few more who have circumnavigated the globe a dozen times before settling down to live five streets or one village away from where they grew up. It may have something to do with the magnetism of family and family ties, but again I know people who have no family who have still been affected by this same curious pattern... so is there something else going on here?

I suspect that there is!

I have begrudgingly come to accept that much as I would rather be living in Andalucia, I am stuck in Britain because this is where I am supposed to be... This is where I will learn the lessons I need to learn (and God knows there are many) and this is where I will be best placed to fulfill my fate and destiny. This is where I will meet the people I need to meet, for their sake and my own, and this is where I shall probably die. I may have some choice in my fate (and I refer you to Sandy's A to B to C theory outlined in chapter three) but ultimately I have no choice in my destiny – and let me go on record in saying that I think fate and destiny are two very different powers, one being the summer breeze that wafts across the cricket fields of Eaton, the other being the tornado that devastates half of a mid-western American state. Both breeze and tornado are wind, but two entirely different manifestations of wind.

You may well ask where I'm going with this conversation and the answer is straight to the Harbour Café down on the cobbled car park that gives access to Bridlington Harbour and the fish quay, which is where I met Sandy for lunch the other day. It was a catch-up time for more questions and answers and time to discuss this whole business of why some places are so important to us while other, sometimes more famous and grandiose places, have no significance. For example, Stonehenge gets all the glory but Avebury has got all the power, while in Glastonbury everyone goes traipsing up the Tor when the epicentre of energy is in the middle of the High Street, just outside the George and Pilgrim Hotel.

Bridlington falls into this category. There are three main

tourist towns on the North Yorkshire coast, and running north to south they are Whitby, Scarborough and Bridlington. Whitby has all the picture postcard views, the cobbled streets and narrow scores and passages; it has the Dracula connection and for more aesthetic tastes it is the old stomping ground of Frank Meadow Sutcliffe, the famous Victorian photographer. Scarborough has the better hotels and bigger and brighter shops, along with more amusement arcades, a couple of night clubs and a half decent theatre. In comparison Bridlington seems to have rather less to offer. For one thing it is more inaccessible than Scarborough and it's not nearly as pretty as Whitby – and yet there is an energy and an atmosphere in Bridlington that the other two towns simply do not have.

You could say this is a subjective matter of opinion and of course you would be right – but only up to a point. Over the last 40 years or so I've taken many friends and acquaintances on the Yorkshire coast tourist trail and those of them who have been psychics, clairvoyants or spiritualists have all, without exception, got the biggest buzz from the Bridlington vibration. I admit to having a family link with Bridlington in the sense that my two godfathers, Kit and John Hastings, were both committed spiritualists and I spent a lot of time as a very small boy in their magical home, then called Villa Bella in Windsor Crescent. Perhaps because of that childhood link Bridlington has always been the place that I run to when I have need of some sea air and solitude. I wouldn't call it my spiritual home – you'd have to travel a couple of thousand miles south to find that sacred place – but it's certainly a point on the map where I can plug in my cable, charge up my batteries and find some fresh energy for the next round of challenges.

I find it to be a happy coincidence that Sandy has a similar view of the town and that back in 1988 the events that caused her to move to the East Yorkshire coast from Lincoln were not in any way accidental but a fine example of spiritual guidance.

1988 was one of those pivotal turning point years for Sandy and it came in the form of two hammer blows. First of all she learned that her friend and favourite Uncle Alan was in hospital suffering from terminal pancreatic cancer and then she was informed that she had Multiple Sclerosis. Either one of these events would have provided food for thought, but both coming together put Sandy and Mike in a position where they did a very rapid reality check.

Mike's business was doing well but even with Sandy's help he was still working 18 hour days and both of their lives revolved and gravitated around their jobs. Any time they had together was the tired time at the end of the day and an occasional Sunday and while Sandy was very happy in her marriage the reality of married family life was far from the pre-conceived idyll. If Alan, who was still only a young man, could suddenly be stricken with a terminal cancer and if Sandy's days were numbered before she became really poorly and had to retreat to the waiting arms of a wheelchair, then what life she had left she was determined to enjoy! Neither she nor Mike made any impulsive moves but they did talk things through at length and they acted very quickly.

Mike closed his business and they sold the house in Little Sokum and together, on a wing and a prayer, they went in search of a new life in the West Country. The plan was that they would find a small cottage somewhere in Devon or Cornwall, Mike would take the first job that came along (and as a qualified marine engineer there was bound to be something) and for as long as she was able, Sandy would carry on doing readings for people.

After quite some time on the West Country property trail without any success she petitioned the spirit world for some help and as usual, the help was forthcoming in a roundabout way. Sandy was sitting in a café and while Mike was reading the local paper she found herself glancing through a property magazine.

And here she found the most perfect property - a small fisherman's cottage, close to the lighthouse with sea views. The only problem was that it was in Bridlington and as anyone will tell you, Bridlington is three hundred miles north east of the West Country.

And yet something immediately clicked in Sandy's mind for her Uncle Alan had been on the point of moving from Derbyshire to East Yorkshire just before he'd been taken ill, and from Sandy's point of view this was Alan pointing the way. So, without even talking about it very much, she and Mike jumped into their car and drove overnight from North Cornwall to East Yorkshire, saw the cottage the following day, and bought it straight away.

In Sandy's own words: "We've lived in a number of houses in Bridlington since then but Brid has always been our home and when we finally moved over here from Lincoln it was really like coming home to the place we were always supposed to be. Living in the north of England isn't perfect, and James, just like you, I'd love a bit more sunshine, but it's been a good place to travel from and I've always had the satisfaction of knowing that this is where spirit brought me, so this is where spirit needs me to be."

It's the middle of August and the rain is pelting down in torrents out of a slate grey sky. We're sitting in the Harbour Café which, while it is not the most salubrious of watering holes, is clean and tidy and they serve a generous cheese burger with double fried chips. Not too good for the waist line but cheering to the soul.

Once upon a time this building was made of wood and it always smelt of damp timber and burnt milk. Someone should have slapped a preservation order on this relic of the 40s and 50s while they still had the chance. Instead, at some point in the early 70s they rebuilt the place with brick and stone and diluted the atmosphere, leaving just a residual psychic echo of an earlier magic. Where once there were little mullioned windows with cheap chintz curtains there is now one big monument to plate glass that gives a stunning view of the harbour. At right angles, a couple of smaller apertures look out onto the dark grey flagstones of the quay. Two couples wrapped in brightly coloured waterproofs, rush through the rain towards the town, heads bowed against the wind. August in England! Ah well…

Whenever I'm in Bridlington I always have a cup of tea in the Harbour Café. I remember my mother taking me there as a child, back in the days when the building was little more than a wooden hut, redolent with the aroma of seaside sand and plastic toys: if Bridlington has a special vibration then for me, the Harbour Café and the smelly old fish quay are both at the very heart of it. I like it better in the mid winter when the tourists are few and the frost is thick: even the worst of the winter storms cannot diminish the inherent energy of the location.

But now it is mid summer and we stare out of the plate glass window at the rain swept view of Bridlington Harbour; it's the height of the tourist season but I have to say there are not too many tourists in sight. There's a high tide and fishing boats and small yachts dance to the gentle swell, halyards clanking above the sound of the hissing hot milk machine behind us. Sandy and I stare at the vista, lost in our own thoughts, thinking of other harbours at other times in other places.

"Mike and I bought a boat once," she remembers out loud. "We saw an advert in a paper… It was going for £2,000 and because of Mike's profession, we bought it sight unseen. We had this lovely thought that we could go down to Majorca where it was moored, do it up, then sail it back to Bridlington. As a back up plan, we reckoned even if it was an absolute wreck we could strip the lead out of the keel and sell it for scrap and get most of our money back."

"So what happened?" I asked, stuffing the last bit of

cheeseburger into my mouth.

She laughed. "Well, we got down to Andraitx where it was berthed and it was in a right old state. All the upper works were in mahogany and the wood wasn't in good condition. The engine was just a mangled block of metal – but it wasn't anything Mike couldn't handle. So we scrubbed and polished and worked away at it, looking forward to the time when we'd be able to sail around the world in search of new adventures. We nearly killed ourselves on at least half a dozen occasions but it was lots of fun.

"Anyway, I remember this occasion when we were just off-shore… there wasn't a breath of wind and the engine had finally given up the ghost for the last time. To our horror we realized we were floating towards this big bank of rocks, so we started yelling and waving our arms, and we set off a flare, and eventually this little man in a small motor boat came and rescued us. He just threw us a line and towed us into Motril harbour and tied us up against the side of this big luxury yacht. No sooner had he gone than we had three guys jumping down onto our deck from the gin palace… They looked very tough and mean and they were waving guns at us… And anyway, to cut a long story short, we'd ended up being moored up against the King of Belgium's yacht.

"This very polite and dignified gentleman, who turned out to be the King, called down to us and told us that we couldn't park our boat there and Mike, totally unfazed, pointed out that we didn't have any choice in the matter because we'd broken down. The King said he quite understood and that he would arrange for a technician to come and sort us out.

"Needless to say we did get it all sorted out eventually and we didn't do much sailing for the rest of that holiday. We had a lovely long conversation with the King and we were all very saddened when this friendly old gentleman died a little while later."

King Baudouin of Belgium died on the 31st July 1993 of

a heart attack while holidaying in his summer residence in Morril and for those of you who find Sandy's story implausible let me assure you it is not. The European monarchy conducts itself rather differently compared with our own Royal Family and I remember an incident years ago when I was mucking about on a boat in the yacht basin at Palma de Mallorca. A couple of guys in swimming trunks hailed me from a Zodiac dinghy and asked me if I had a light for a cigarette. I obliged by chucking my old Zippo down to the taller of the two men in the dinghy who lit his cigarette, then tossed the lighter back with a salute and a wave then revved off towards a very beautiful boat about a hundred metres distant.

"Do you know who that was?" asked the Spanish colleague I was working with at the time.

"No, who was it?" I replied.

"That was Juan Carlos!"

"Juan Carlos who?"

"Juan Carlos, the King of Spain, you idiot!"

Later that same day as I was strolling along the Paseo Maritimo I saw a very sleek launch unloading its passengers at the quay side and, sure enough, the fellow in the neatly tailored trousers and sports shirt was clearly Juan Carlos, King of Spain. Little wonder I had failed to recognise him in his swimming trunks and wrap around sunglasses. You don't expect to meet kings in Zodiac dinghies looking for a light for their cigarettes!

No, you don't expect to meet kings in swimming trunks and nor do you expect to be told, when you're still only 41, that you have MS. Sandy may have had her highs, such as the episode with King Baudouin of Belgium but, God knows, she had her lows as well.

From 1988 onwards she was in an increasing degree of pain and discomfort as the disease took hold; she battled against constant fatigue and sometimes her joints and muscles were so tight and stiff that she could hardly raise her head from her pillow. There were many days when she couldn't walk and Mike had to push her around in a wheelchair and although there were times when she must have been profoundly depressed, especially with the onset on Sjogren's Syndrome which saps all the moisture from the body causing a dry mouth and dry eyes, Sandy fought on and took some solace from her belief that she was experiencing what she was supposed to be experiencing and despite her discomfort she was on the pre-arranged pathway ordained by Spirit.

...And I'm sure that it was the same Spirit that inspired her to fight back. She read and researched every piece of information available on the disease and started paying a great deal of attention to her diet. She initiated a programme of mental and physical exercises that she kept to religiously and with great effort throughout, she applied an attitude of mind over matter and did her best to maintain a positive mental attitude. She believes it is this last factor that began to turn the tide. Slowly but surely some of her worst symptoms began to dissipate until the day she made a formal contract with the spirit world... She would continue to keep a wheelchair in the house on condition that Spirit kept her out of it!

Sandy was diagnosed with MS at the age of 41 and at the time of writing she is now 64. For the last 23 years her prescription of self help seems to be working very well. She still suffers from chronic fatigue (although you'd never think so to look at her) and she has to use eye drops six times a day to stay on top of the Sjogren's Syndrome, but every time I see her she is effervescent with the spirit of life and a joie de vivre which is positively infectious. At only four feet and eleven inches she is a little blond bombshell of positive energy which touches and lifts all those who come into contact with her.

Fighting through the pain of her illness Sandy found a degree of spiritual maturity and along with that maturity a degree of confidence that enabled her to start asking questions of Spirit. Not questions like "what is the meaning of life" or "what will next week's winning lottery numbers be" but key questions that could provide proof of life after death to the people who found their way to her door…

"James, it's the little things that count… Being able to come up with a name, for example, so I always ask for a name. Apart from anything else, I need to know who I'm talking to and instead of saying to someone 'I've got a lovely old gentleman here with a bald head and a fat belly' it's so much better, so much more evidential, to say 'I've got your Grandfather with me and he's telling me that his name is Arnold.' Now, if the person I'm sitting with never had a Grandfather called Arnold, I've got it wrong and I've got to go back to spirit and try again. But if they *did* have a Grandfather and his name *was* Arnold then that's my green light to pass go.

"I always make it crystal clear to my sitters that I'm not a fortune teller. My job is to prove post mortem survival. I tell them that I'm not always in charge of my own mouth because when spirit is communicating with me they seem to bypass the brain and go straight to the vocal chords… So sometimes a name, especially a name that sounds the same, can get a bit muddled up. I always have a problem with the J's – is it Jack, John or Jim? And the M's give me some headaches… Is it Margaret, Marjory or Mary? Sometimes I'll just get the 'Maar' on the tip of my tongue and have got to work it out from there. We usually get there in the end, and once I've made a link with one person from the spirit world there's invariably another dozen waiting to come through. That's why some of my readings seem to go on for ever, and that's why that lot waiting Upstairs…" she points upwards towards the ceiling of the Harbour Café… "can sometimes get so impatient."

Upstairs. I smile quietly to myself because this is a place that we all have our own favourite name for. Sandy calls it Upstairs, some older spiritualists call it The Summerlands, ardent Christians will refer to it as Heaven, Pagan Vikings would have called it Valhalla. Bottom line is that it's the place that we go to – or at least the place that *our spirits* go to – when we die.

And when we start thinking about this particular subject it brings us very much to the heart of the matter. If there is life after death, what form does it take? If heaven exists, where exactly is it and who's in charge? Are there separate heavens for Christians, Muslims and Jews?

I share my thoughts with Sandy. She has a fit of the giggles (which I don't find particularly illuminating) and then gives me a rather sad look.

"Oh James, I wish I had all the answers for you, I really do. What you've got to remember is that I'm just one little person working away on her own pathway. I'm no great expert or guru and I can only tell you what spirit has told me when I've asked the same kind of questions. Basically, the spirit world is whatever you perceive it to be. Whatever you *need* it to be!"

She has my full attention because what she is saying coincides with my own views, expressed in my book "Survival" (Mage Publishing) and confirmed to some extent by the subject of that book, Stephen Holbrook. So I revisit that theme and theory.

"In other words," I choose my words very carefully, "if my idea of heaven is a golden beach with bright blue skies and palm trees with Bacardi on tap and pretty girls in hula hula skirts, that's what I'm likely to find?"

"Pretty much."

"And the housewife who's idea of heaven is a huge shopping mall full of designer goods and a golden piece of plastic with an unlimited line of credit – that's what she's going to find when *she* crosses over to the other side?"

"Yes, but James, think on. Both you and the housewife are going to get pretty bored after a while and you're going to start looking for other things so I suspect that the golden beach and the shopping mall are only temporary residences until you feel that it's time to move on to something else."

"What else?"

"You tell me… No, I mean it, James. You tell me what you might think you'd like to do once you get over to the world of spirit, or go "upstairs" as I put it."

I thought about it for a while and oddly enough it wasn't a very long list, but long or short, it wasn't feasible until another related matter was settled.

"It would depend," I said slowly, "on the matter of identity. If, when I pass over, I'm just going to be absorbed into a block of spirit like a bee in a hive, then there isn't very much I *could* do. If, on the other hand, I retain my *identity* and all of the memories from the life I've just lived, well that would be an entirely different matter…"

"Of course we retain our identities, James! If we didn't how would mediums be able to channel any of the messages they get? And what's more, you don't just retain your identity and memories of the life you've just lived, you're given access to all the memories and lessons you've learned from the lives you've lived before."

"What happens if I haven't had any previous lives?"

"Well, bearing in mind that reincarnation is an option and not an obligation, it could be said that you were starting right at the very beginning of your pathway." I think she could sense that this subject troubled me and her voice softened. "There's one thing I can promise you, and that is when you get to the other side you'll be exactly the same as you are now, only nicer, younger and healthier. You will be the person you'd like to see yourself as being."

Sandy's last sentence caused a deep resonance in the seat of my soul. *"You will be the person you'd like to see yourself as being!"*

This made perfect sense to me for when I see my Grandmother in my dreams and visions I do not see her as the ancient 96 year old husk that she became just before she died, but as the sprightly 60 year old who looked after me in loco parentis when I was a young boy. When I see dead friends, I see them as being much younger and more vibrant than they were when I knew them in life. There is a simple message here somewhere. It is obtuse, but nevertheless reassuring.

Sandy cocks her head to one side as though listening to an invisible third party, then she looks me directly in the eye. "So, what *would* you do, once you'd passed over and had got bored with your golden beach and Bacardi on tap?"

"I would try to make reparation for all the things I'd done wrong and got wrong in this life… I'd try to help all those people I'd hurt and if I couldn't do much to help them, at least I'd like to say sorry for all the mistakes that I've made."

I shuffle uncomfortably and then, somewhat embarrassed about the intimate direction of our conversation, I glance at my watch. We've been in the café for more than an hour and it's time to move on to another subject.

"Tell me," I suggest "about the psychic art. How did it start? Where did it come from?"

"James, I hardly know where to begin!"

Longing for the pipe I no longer smoke, or at least a cigarette, I tell her to begin at the beginning.

Six: Doodles and Stephen Holbrook

In the depths of the Multiple Sclerosis and with the onset of osteoporosis Sandy would frequently fall and break a bone; all she need do was stub a toe against the leg of a table and the toe would break, but her indomitable will and stoicism kept her going. In her mind, she foresaw the day when her legs would pack up altogether and she would become permanently confined to her wheelchair. "Never mind," she thought. "I can still read and write and I can still sew and make dresses" and on the tail end of those thoughts came another. "One day," she said to herself, "I'd really love to learn how to draw."

Undeterred by the fact that her sight was very poor, she nevertheless tried her hand at sketching and the results left much to be desired. "You need to see what you're trying to draw," she told me. "You can't just draw what you feel. And in those days, before I had the laser surgery on my eyes, I could hardly see my hand in front of my face." In the end, totally defeated by her childlike doodles, she reluctantly gave up on her quest and concentrated on other things that *did* bring some success and reward. By this time, she had built up a solid reputation as a medium and there was always a stream of people making their way to her door. She did her readings for donations only, and although she was popular, she certainly wasn't getting rich.

And then, one day while she was casually walking through the town centre, she came upon a young street artist sketching a portrait. Looking over his shoulder she was totally blown away by the young man's work and found herself thinking "Oh, I really must have another go at doing this!" She found herself in conversation with the artist and asked if he might be available to give her some lessons. The young man said he'd be happy to give it a try and visited Sandy's home on half a dozen occasions. Each time, she watched him work and learned some basic sketching techniques using the grid system. While the artist was there to encourage her she made a small amount of progress and then for whatever reason he stopped coming and Sandy's meagre talents seem to have deserted her completely. She still tried to get something down on paper but by her own admission "…it was hopeless and I had to face the sad truth of the matter, which was that I simply couldn't draw!"

Some people, Sandy included, are doodlers and while on the telephone, or listening to the radio or watching TV, Sandy would doodle away with a pencil using whatever scrap of paper came to hand. Sometimes it might be the back of an envelope and other times the margin of the local newspaper. Frequently she could be watching a television programme and have no idea at the end of it what it had been all about but when it came to tidying up the odd bits of paper she'd been scribbling on she had got into the habit of putting them on a small coffee table at the end of the sofa. Frequently, especially if it was late in the evening, she wouldn't even bother looking at them until the following morning.

One particular night she'd stood up to stretch her legs and visit the bathroom: as she turned towards the door she noticed some movement from the little pile of paper on the coffee table. There were no sudden gusts of wind, no vortex caused by Sandy's action of standing up (which was something she did very slowly and carefully) and to Sandy's eyes the sheaves of paper which contained her doodles and sketches moved entirely of their own volition. When she looked down at the table, more in curiosity than amazement, she did so to find a pair of eyes staring up at her from one of her drawings…

Sandy – "It was a pair of totally real, totally human eyes and as I moved around the end of the sofa to get a better look it was as though the eyes followed me every step of the way! I called Mike over to have a look, but he didn't seem either bothered or impressed…"

Mike explained to me that one of the reasons why he was so casual about the incident was that for weeks previously he'd been walking around the house picking up screwed up scraps of paper that contained "quite accurate" sketches of noses, mouths, eyes and ears. Understandably he couldn't quite figure out why Sandy was suddenly getting so excited.

For Sandy, however, something had clicked and had fallen into place. Initially in the form of an experiment, she got herself a proper sketch pad and some pencils, then found a quiet corner of the house. Taking the pencil in her hand, she sat at a table and closed her eyes, waiting to see if anything would happen. She didn't have to wait very long and within seconds she was aware of the pencil flying across the paper. She neither felt nor sensed some spectral hand pushing the pencil on her behalf but she was absolutely clear that she wasn't moving the pencil on her own. Less than a minute after the process had begun Sandy looked down at the page of her sketch pad and instead of just a nose or an ear or an eye, she found a fully formed face staring up at her.

Sandy would be the first to admit that this drawing was no great work of art. In many ways, it was crude and raw, but it was the first time she had sketched a fully formed face and it was superior in every way to anything she had previously attempted. She says: "It was far beyond my talents as an artist because I didn't have any talent as an artist and I knew with total certainty that although it might have been my hand that had been holding the pencil and moving across the paper, it wasn't really me who'd drawn the picture. Someone else had been using me as the channel."

Sandy may not have studied at Oxford or Cambridge but she'd graduated with honours from the University of Life. She is a clever and intelligent woman and although she'd had no direct contact with the phenomena, she'd heard of psychic artists and was familiar with the concept of automatic writing, which is where a clairvoyant will sit with pen and paper and allow Spirit to channel information through in the form of the written word. She knew that something important was happening here and although she'd been in touch with the world of spirit all of her life she sensed that this sudden proclivity towards art marked a major change in the direction of her mediumship.

This belief was confirmed a very short while later. She was sitting in the hairdressing salon sketching on her pad (which she now took everywhere with her) when the hairdresser looked over her shoulder to see what she was doing – and let out a very loud gasp.

"Oh my God," she exclaimed. "That's my Granddad!"

Although Sandy had not had any connection with the first face she had drawn, the incident with the hairdresser seemed to suggest that she was drawing the faces of people who had passed over into spirit. Over the following weeks this was confirmed on countless occasions when people would look at Sandy's sketches and tell her that she had drawn their mother or their father, their son or daughter or brother. There was a double dose of satisfaction for Sandy in this, emanating from the joyful reaction she got from people who saw her bring their loved ones back to life, albeit on the pages of a sketch pad, and also from the sure-fire knowledge that she was providing visual proof of post mortem survival. After all, she reasoned, a picture is worth a thousand words!

A little while after that Sandy was leafing through her local newspaper which in itself was a rare occurrence because she ardently loathes and hates the things – "…they're so often full of dirt and despair and lots of nasty stories that hurt people and destroy lives…" when quite by accident she came across a small advertisement which said that international medium Stephen Holbrook was visiting Scarborough in the very near future. She immediately felt a closing sensation with her spirit guide who told her that she had to go to this evening and without really thinking about it, she phoned up and booked the tickets.

Nearer to the evening of clairvoyance she again felt the tingling cool/warm sensation that always came when her guide came in really close.

"Sandy, you must take your sketch pad with you!"

The message from her guide caused horror and her initial reaction was to think no chance, no way! She simply couldn't go along to an evening organized by one of the nation's leading mediums and take a sketch pad. What on earth would he think? What would his audience think? This was his evening, not hers. However, her guide was insistent *"Sandy, you must take your sketch pad"* and the argument went back and forth right up until the 11th hour, at which time Sandy did a deal, both with spirit and with herself. She would take the sketch pad, but it would stay firmly tucked into her shoulder bag *unless* circumstance conspired to conjure up a situation where she could meet the medium alone for a few minutes prior to the demonstration. If such an opportunity presented itself she would approach him and tell him who she was, and ask him if he'd mind if she sat at the back of the room and did a few drawings while he worked. She was desperate to discover if she could make a connection with another medium, and more importantly, to the spirit people he himself would be connecting with over the course of the evening. Armed with a picture that she had already drawn that would, she'd been informed by her guide, connect with someone she would meet at Stephen Holbrook's demonstration, she and Mike arrived very early at Scarborough's Royal Hotel...

And this is a very good time and place to shift the focus of this writing because for the sake of clarity and context I need to speak a little about Stephen Holbrook.

I met Stephen in April of 1999 and that meeting led to an exciting and highly rewarding association that lasted for 11 years. At various times I acted as promoter, tour manager and biographer and always felt very secure in these roles because I knew I was working with someone who was totally honest and sincere in his commitment towards spiritualism. The fact that he was without doubt the best medium I'd ever met in 30 years also helped a bit. In short, Stephen Holbrook was the real deal.

Just like Sandy, Stephen's psychic abilities made their presence felt very early in his life but unlike Sandy he had to battle long and hard to recognise and come to terms with what was happening to him.

Also, just like Sandy (and most other mediums as well) he came from an ordinary working class background without any illusions, delusions or pretensions of grandeur. He started attending the spiritualist church in his late teens, was not particularly impressed with some of the mediums who were on the church circuit at the time, and felt that he could do better himself.

Putting his money where his mouth was, he tested this theory in lots of small venues in central Yorkshire and even before the age of 20 had built up an enviable reputation. Stephen trained to be a hairdresser and indeed was a hairdresser for many years, seeing clients during the course of the day and then rushing off all over the county to do his clairvoyant demonstrations in the evening. This led to a lifestyle of 16 or 17 hour days six and sometimes seven days a week while at the same time trying to be a good husband and bringing up three children.

This was the status quo of Stephen's life when I first met him and I'd like to think that eleven years, three books and one thousand venues later I might have helped him move on a little bit. Having shunned the temptation of lucrative television shows he may not be the best known medium in the land but he is cerainly one of the busiest and when a guy called Harry Andrews who is the doyen of the psychic scene and spiritualist movement n the USA described Stephen as "the most gifted young medium demonstrating in Britain today" he did, I believe, get it absolutely right.

Stephen is one of those modest men who knows a lot more han he thinks he knows. His judgement in matters temporal may be a matter of subjective taste – for years he had an ongoing love affaire with an old red Austin Montego – but his instincts and judgement in matters spiritual are unquestionable. With these thoughts in mind, I would like to present you with Stephen's account of his first meeting with Sandy which gives another insight to this remarkable lady from a third party's point of view.

Stephen Holbrook's Evidence

"It was December 2008 and I was so looking forward to my last demonstration of the year which happened to be in Scarborough. This is always the case at this time of year; I love my job with a passion that only I would understand, but it had been a very long year, and I was weary to say the least! It was a terrible night, foggy and rainy, and what should have been an hour's drive from home had turned into a two hour nightmare!

"We pulled up in front of the Royal Hotel, ready to start unloading all the paraphernalia that we need for a demo, and we were trying to be as quick as we could before the traffic wardens spotted us! Rob *(Steve's manager. Ed)* and I have a system of unpacking and repacking the car – sometimes it looks like a challenge from the Krypton Factor – and we were on our second trip into the function room when I was stopped by an immaculately dressed woman who I initially thought was a resident of the hotel. However, to my surprise, she was a very early member of the audience, it was only 6pm, and we didn't start for another hour and a half.

"She proceeded to tell me that she was a psychic artist called Sandy Ingham, and she was looking forward to the evening. In the past, I have had experiences with psychic artists, none of them very good experiences I must admit – the portraits I had seen were poor classroom attempts of faces, they really could have been anybody they were so vague. I mention this only because it had tainted my views and I do, as my Granddad always said, call a spade a shovel. For those who are not from Yorkshire, this means I say what I mean!

"So, to say I was a little dubious was an understatement, and I really showed little enthusiasm to the lady, but was very diplomatic in my response and I thought I handled it very well, although I have since found out from Sandy she knew exactly what I was thinking – how embarrassing! – but she didn't let on. That evening, Sandy had with her a portrait she had done earlier in the day and said it would be placed that night to a member of the audience. Admittedly the picture was beautifully drawn, but I hadn't seen Sandy physically do it, and for all I knew, she could have spent days doing it, or even copied it. In any event, I advised Sandy to wait in the bar area until we were ready to open, and wondered exactly what she wanted from the evening.

"On the 3rd and last visit to the car, I was accosted again by two more early arrivals for the demonstration; they had arrived early just to make sure they were in the right place as we usually used the St Nicholas Hotel. I advised them to also sit in the bar, and we would call them through when the doors opened.

"Most mediums tend to disappear before a show to distance themselves away from the hubbub of an arriving audience, wanting to instill peace and calm, and perhaps meditate. I can't do that, I just get on with it, putting out flyers or posters, helping with seating, or chatting to people who speak to me on the way in. I'd rather be busy, it helps me to stop being nervous. However, being in broad view of everyone before the demo does have its perils, as people do often come and think they are the only person there, and drain you before you start, asking lots and lots of questions. It is nice that people feel I am approachable, but when you have to be on top form, it is hard work to be drained before you start.

"Shortly after the doors were open, I saw Sandy and Mike, her husband, in the queue, together with the two 'early bird' ladies who seemed to be in a state of shock but very elated. Sandy explained that when the two ladies came into the bar they sat next to Sandy (who happened to have the picture she had drawn earlier on the table in front her), and they gasped when they saw the picture. They asked how on earth she got it, as it was a portrait of their mother! One of them proceeded to get out of her handbag an identical photograph of her mum that she had brought along just in case it may help her get a message. When I looked and compared the two pictures, it wasn't just the lady who was in shock, it was absolutely amazing!

"Now, I'm the first to admit that when I'm not engaged with the spirit world, I'm not psychic, my awareness is often more lacking than most, and that's not just my opinion, but the opinion of many that know me! So, often my first impressions fail me wildly and I started to think that maybe, just maybe, this could be the start of something really spiritually special, but I didn't know exactly what. And, of course, being a Taurean, I was still unsure about the whole thing.

"Then again, being a man of many contradictions, unlike a Taurean, I can be quite spontaneous, and can arrive at decisions quite quickly, so just as I was walking down the aisle to start the evening I quickly said to Sandy – totally out of the blue – 'Would you like to draw whilst I demonstrate?' to which she readily agreed and sat almost at the front of the audience where there happened to be a couple of spare seats. To be quite honest, when I'm on stage and tuned in, I am aware of very little of what is happening around me, apart from the person I am talking to, so the first half of the evening started and finished as usual after about 50 minutes, though it always seems to me to be only 10 minutes.

"After I had finished what was an extremely emotional first half, mainly taken up by a large family of seven, nearly at the back of the audience – they had lost an aunt the day before, a young gentleman who was killed in Ireland, also the mother of the family and another gentleman who I believe was the grandfather – who received absolute proof of the existence of their loved ones, I had a flash of inspiration! If Sandy had done any drawings at all, surely at least one would be of this family's relatives. I quickly rushed over and asked Sandy if the people could see the drawings she had done and, lo and behold, each of their family members had been drawn by Sandy whilst I was demonstrating. The family were absolutely amazed and so happy that there was an extra piece of proof. Sandy had no idea who these people were, where they were sat, and especially had no clue who their relatives were! She was at the front of the room facing me, and had no idea who I was talking to, and I know Sandy drops into her own little world when she is drawing so had no awareness of who or what is around her.

"Oh dear! I seemed to have misjudged a situation again! I knew this, but was extremely excited, emotional, and felt as though someone had messed with my head! This certainly wasn't what I was expecting from the last demo of the year before a well earned rest! I think it fair to say that until that point, I had made it clear to Sandy that I had been more than impressed by what I had witnessed. The portraits were beautifully done, each one in a matter of minutes, and I have often said to people since, if you were watching a street artist doing a copy portrait, you would expect to wait at least 30 minutes. Now, I'm no expert, but I feel that I can draw on a little knowledge gained during my two year combined arts course (which I passed with distinction, incidentally) to know that these were good. I've always been artistic, but never really academic, and I could clearly see these portraits were easily identifiable as being the same people I had communicated with. They were all completely different and unique.

"I knew, as I said, these portraits were good, but didn't know what to do next. I withdrew into my little shell as I needed lots of time to think about it. I also let Sandy know my feelings too, that I don't rush into things. Everything I've ever done has been thought through in great detail first, especially when it comes to involving other people in my work. I said to Sandy that I would take her telephone number and would ring her within six weeks. That would give me enough time to think and get Christmas, New Year, and our imminent Clairvoyance Cruise out of the way. Things are busy enough then with family and work commitments, without bombarding my brain with extra workload!

"After saying our goodbye's I got into the car and on the way explained to Rob what I had witnessed. Rob is my sounding board for many ideas and thoughts, and I take on board what he says before making any decision. Although he had not been in the demo itself, he had seen the portraits and the look on the peoples' faces as they saw them. He was very impressed, but wasn't really in a position to make a decision either as he was as exhausted as I was! I did, however, assure Sandy by text that I had enjoyed meeting her and Mike, I'd been blown away and I would ring her when I said I would and discuss things further. I then promptly fell asleep – rest assured, Rob was driving!

"Between Christmas and the cruise, I had told several people about Sandy's talent as I was still so impressed, even weeks after the event! I do naturally believe that Spirit put things into place for a reason, and what is meant to be, will be. So after six weeks as promised, I rang Sandy and asked her if she wanted to do a couple of my evenings as a 'special guest'. She was happy to oblige and we both went in to the first evening excited and a little unsure of how it would work out! I wondered how it would compare to the first evening in Scarborough, but I needn't have worried. By the end of the night Sandy had rattled off at least eight portraits, all of which were readily taken up by the stunned audience. My God, I thought, this really does work! We were both impressed by how well we had worked together, and thanked our little spirit 'helpers'.

"From then on, Sandy and I worked together at least a couple of times a week, all over the UK, and slowly but surely, the portraits became even more 'alive' if you'll pardon the pun. They weren't just portraits, it seemed to me, but actual people wanting to jump off the page and get the validation from their loved one. Sandy, being a medium herself, would also draw little pictures at the bottom of the sheet, like a rose, or a baby rattle, or even simply a date, but always something that meant that little extra something to the people involved. People who had only died recently, as well as those who had been passed on for years. Amazing! Sometimes when I have finished the first or second half, Sandy is still half way through a portrait, but has the ability to say which one of my audience members it is for. Even when it is half completed, the person can tell who it is straight away, and often say 'oh my God, its mum!' They wait patiently until Sandy has finished, and it is even more astonishing. Sandy has often drawn two separate portraits at the same time, one with her left hand and one with the right, and they are completely differ-ent. One can be a small baby, and the other can be a very distin-guished older gentleman with a moustache and hat. The link is that they both belong to the person receiving the message. It is amazing to see.

"And now, we are in December 2010, how quick time flies, it's unbelievable. The past two years have been a special chapter in my life, our relationship as two people has developed and a spiritual bond and friendship has grown which I will always value. On a parallel spiritual level, our two respective guides appear to have linked forces, and work as well together as Sandy and I do. The portraits were more linked to the messages than ever, and people all over the UK, and on the Caribbean Cruise, were constantly impressed.

"My mediumship has taken many turns over the 20 years or so, some of them have been wrong turns, but you expect that along the way, but if anyone had said to me three years previously that I would be working alongside a psychic artist in the future, I would certainly have thought they'd gone mad! However, it does prove my theory that our lives are like a jigsaw puzzle. There are hundreds of pieces, not all of which we can see, but they will eventually fall into place bit by bit as our lives progress, until we eventually see the whole image. I do think that when I met Sandy it was another part of my jigsaw that I had not foreseen. It taught me a lesson that when Spirit have plans for us, it is for a reason and we shouldn't fight it. It has been a valuable journey of discovery for us both, two very different instruments coming together making a wonderful piece of music.

"I'd like to share something with you. Many people over the years have said that they were thrilled they had received a message, that it was very comforting and reassuring, but they want to know if I get messages for myself? Well, I never have and I just take it as read that it's my job to pass my gift to others. To this day, nothing ever comes to me, for me. But one night in Hull, working at the Quality Hotel with Sandy, I had just reached over to one of Sandy's portraits to pass on to a lady, and I just stood there speechless – highly unusual as most will know! Sandy had drawn a portrait of a very dear friend of mine, Terry Sutton, who had passed on some time ago. He was the kind man who helped me get started many years ago. He was a total sceptic initially until he sat through some of the demonstrations, and he became a firm believer and found it fascinating. Terry's lovely wife, Eileen, and her family always came to see me, but this was the first time she had seen Sandy, or any psychic artist for that matter. I stared at the portrait of Terry and it threw me, I had to carry on somehow until the end of the first half. I managed it somehow, then rushed over to Eileen, portrait in hand, to show her. She was dumbstruck, and then true to form, pulled out of her handbag the picture she always carries, and it was *exactly* like the portrait. It was as if Terry was giving me the blessing that Sandy and I working together was meant to be and, bless his heart, letting me know he was still there giving a helping hand.

"So, Sandy Ingham, I have to say that you are one of the *very* few people who can render me speechless! I only wish that you can find a window of opportunity worthy of the valuable and phenomenal work that you do, in the hope that these portraits that you produce - with the breathtaking help of your guide – can be seen by many many more people. Instruments like you do not come along in life very often. I am one person who values the work you do a thousand percent. The only other people who could be as passionate about your work are the multitude of people who have received one of your portraits of someone who has so often been taken away from them so cruelly.

"Here's to a long and continued friendship, and I hope the journey we share is a safe and rewarding one.

Love Steve…"

I'd like to thank Stephen for his exceptionally valuable input and close this section of the book with one small piece of corroborative evidence. The gentleman called Terry Sutton that Steve mentioned is someone that I did not know well, but I did meet him on half a dozen occasions and was deeply impressed by his warmth and hospitality. I was very sad to hear of his passing. He had a very distinct face, full of character and good humour, and the photographer in me would have loved to photograph him, probably low key in living black and white. When I was shown Sandy's portrait of Terry there was absolutely no doubt in my mind that this was definitely a picture of Terry Sutton. The detail was quite incredible, even down to the mole on his cheek and slightly gappy teeth.

Seven: An Argument

By virtue of the fact you are reading this book, I think it can be safely assumed that you might have some interest in the subjects of spiritualism and life after death. Perhaps you are looking for an affirmation of an existing belief or perhaps you are just searching for more information – more evidence – before you come to a definitive conclusion.

I think that before any such conclusion can be reached there must be a rigorous examination of the evidence, not particularly by the laws of science but by the laws of common sense. I set this criterion because in my opinion science and, by definition, scientists know very little about what is and what is not real. They may, for example, be able to measure the speed of the wind but they have no idea what colour it might be. They are convinced that our universe started with a big bang, but ask them what was there before the big bang or who lit the fuse that caused the explosion – and all you get for your trouble is a blank look. They cleverly dismiss the question as irrelevant because they haven't got a clue what the answer might be. The scientist's view that something cannot be real until it can be identified, measured and replicated is, on one side of the coin, quite funny but, on the other side of the coin, it is an expression of the most incredible arrogance and is absolutely breath-taking.

Science is so sure that it has all the answers that it frequently misses the glaringly obvious. For example, I am writing this on the 23rd of September 2011 and it has just been announced that Einstein's theorem of E=MC^2 – the theory that says that nothing can travel faster than the speed of light – might actually not be the case. If this is so, it invalidates every theory, every experiment, every philosophy, every lesson, every textbook, every discussion and every argument science has put forward on the subject over the last 100 years. Shocking! The laws of physics will have to be changed and the rule books re-written.

I suspect that this would not surprise old Albert one jot for in an unguarded moment he was heard to say *"I am enough of an artist to draw freely on my imagination. Imagination is more important than knowledge. Knowledge is limited while imagination encircles the world."*

And yet, here's the thing. $E=MC^2$ has always been a flawed theorem because there has always been something that can travel faster than the speed of light, and that something is human thought. Shamans and mystics have always known this truth and the student of military history might be interested to learn that at the height of the cold war the Soviet Union spent a lot of time and some vast amounts of very serious money experimenting with thought transference techniques and various aspects and applications of mental telepathy.

I have argued with many scientists over the years and have patiently pointed out that, even if one looks at the subject of spiritualism from a scientific point of view, while there is a huge volume of evidence for life after death going back over many thousands of years to the civilisations of Babylon and Sumeria and beyond, there is absolutely no evidence for *no* life after death. Science contests this argument by saying you cannot prove the non-existence of something which does not exist. It is a clever answer, but totally disingenuous.

You're walking down the road. Thick black smoke is billowing out of the windows of a house. Do you have to see the flames to know that the house is on fire?

Your ship has struck an iceberg and is sinking fast. Half the boat is already under water. Do you have to get your feet wet to know it's time to abandon ship?

The point that I am trying to make here is that there is a

phenomenal record of evidence for post mortem survival that has been gathered, recorded, collated and absorbed into just about every culture and religious faith imaginable since the beginning of time. Indeed, in most cases, regardless of your vision of God, the belief in an afterlife has become the cornerstone of most faith systems. Thus, if science denies the possibility of a spiritual afterlife, science is also denying the existence of God. If science then goes on to dismiss the possibility of communication between the world of the living and the world of the dead, it is conveniently ignoring the validity of every religious treatise ever written, including the contents of the Christian Bible and the Muslim Koran not to mention half a million other recorded affirmations that never found their way into these holy books. In short, science not only denies spiritualism, it also denies the existence of Spirit within Man.

The scientific riposte is to say that God exists only within the minds of men because, fearful of his own mortality, Man *needs* to believe in the existence of God. Therefore, rather than God creating Man in his own image, Man has created God in *Man's* own image. This is a valid point of view, but it is only a point of view, not only unproven but also unexamined, and it should not in any circumstances be presented as a matter of fact.

When I ask my scientist friends how they explain the phenomena of messages received from beyond the grave, they respond by speaking of many different things such as Man's gullibility and his need to believe in something other than his own puny self. They speak of fraudulent mediums, of plants in the audience – and by following this line of reasoning they inadvertently ally themselves with the philosophy expounded by the Christian church which dictates that the only way to God is through the teachings of Jesus Christ – never mind that Christianity is a minority faith when compared with Islam, Hinduism and Buddhism. How ironic that, in the process of denial, science has formed an alliance with one of the most supposedly spiritual organisations in the western world – an organisation that claims to be spiritual but damns and defames spiritualism! This is doubly ironic because spiritualism is the only religious movement that can actually provide hard evidence for the continuation of spirit after death. One would have thought that an alliance between Christians and Spiritualists was more logical (and beneficial) than an alliance between the church and science... But consider this; senior churchmen and senior scientists have one vital common bond. They are all members of the establishment and it is very much to their advantage that the boat should not be rocked! If a religious alternative undermines the authority of the church, then the priesthood is threatened. If science is proven to be flawed (as it has been on so very many occasions) then the dons and doyens of science can kiss their pensions and positions of power and influence goodbye. I look forward to the day when it might happen. If nothing else, it might wipe those smug expressions of unassailable self-satisfaction from their faces.

I find myself asking why there cannot be a sympathetic symbiosis between the Christian church and spiritualism. It is, as I've said, a logical union. I suppose it's because if you're Mr Tesco, the only supermarket in a small town, you certainly don't want Mr Sainsbury opening up on your doorstep and muscling in on your territory. Your monopoly is destroyed, your profitability is threatened. And sadly, although there are many individuals within the church who work unstintingly for the betterment of Man, the Christian church never was, and is even less so today, a *spiritual* organisation.

Even if we ignore the long term history of the church stretching back over the last two thousand years – two thousand years of torture, conquest, conflict and repression – and focus on the last hundred years or so of infamy and betrayal, it seems to me that the church in general, and the Catholic church in particular, has lost all moral authority. Again, only in my opinion, it is no longer in any position to preach and it should keep its sancti-monious mouth shut until it has put its own house in order.

As a practising psychic and occasional Pagan I have come in for my fair share of flack over the years. In the earlier days of his work, Stephen Holbrook occasionally had to face hostile crowds outside one or two of his venues – never more than half a dozen placards gathered around a dog collar – and Sandy has also had to deal with the ugly faces of bigotry and ignorance. Frankly, anyone who stands apart from the crowd is viewed with suspicion. We get used to it. We are saddened by it, but at least we understand it and that makes it a little easier to deal with.

Scientist and sceptic demand hard proof that the medium's claims are valid but what event or occurrence could be accepted as proof? There is a mass of evidence that is most certainly more than just circumstantial and has been gathered and collated from many different sources over many long years, but science insists that this is just circumstantial evidence and *not* hard proof. When a medium fails to make a spiritual contact either in a laboratory or a TV studio, it is no use claiming that the atmosphere is wrong or that the surroundings are too sterile: science has its victory in the medium's inability to perform in this environment and any-thing the medium or clairvoyant might say in their self defence is greeted with contempt and derision.

Reverse the situation, however, and one wonders how effective the scientist might be in reproducing some scientific experiment *out* of his normal environment with a dozen people looking over his shoulder willing him to make a mistake, and even the non-scientific sceptic might have some difficulty per-forming some deeply personal and intimate act in front of an expectant audience.

As any clairvoyant or medium will tell you, the process of forging a link between Man and Spirit is very natural. It is not an energy that can be turned on and off like a tap – although there are a number of techniques that a medium will use to tune in to the world of spirit and let the people "upstairs" or on the "other side" know that there are loved ones on the earth plane waiting to communicate. It is a personal process, a deeply emotional process, and something which is profoundly spiritual in its nature. You can't put this in a test tube and measure it. You can't weigh it on a set of scales. For the scientist or the sceptic to understand what is going on here they must be brave enough to remove the white coat of preconceived conviction and the bottle neck glasses of bigotry. If they can open their minds to humanity and just for a moment break free from the restrictions imposed by their training – and in many cases, their fear – then they might have a chance of connecting with that inner core of themselves that some people call the soul, and begin to understand what is happening when Man and Spirit make contact through the veil that separates life from death.

I suppose the ultimate proof would be if everyone on the planet experienced an irrefutable contact with the spirit world at more or less the same time. That would put an end to all argument and remove the need to evaluate evidence. The truth would be there for all to see. Maybe such an event, if it ever happened, would constitute The Day of Judgement, referenced not only in the Bible but in most other religious writings as well.

As a defence against the two specific attacks made against clairvoyants and spiritualism – namely that people who believe in these things are delusional and that clairvoyants and mediums have plants secreted in their audiences, on the first indictment science does have a valid point because it is true that some people will believe anything (especially if they are being asked to believe in something that sounds good). However, to accuse everyone who has ever received a message from a departed loved one as being self-deluded is highly insulting and totally irrational. We may be vulnerable in our grief but that vulnerability frequently heightens and hones our powers of perception. Science does not take into consideration the strength of human emotion and it is this very same human emotion that enhances our receptiveness and our ability to tune into a higher and always different level of human awareness. Spiritualism is not an evangelical faith. It follows a very gentle live and let live kind of philosophy, an "each to his own" attitude which is just about as unaggressive and non-threatening as you can get. It is curious then to ponder and ask why it warrants such virulent attacks from the establishment. Could it be, perhaps, that by presenting proof of an afterlife it undermines the authority of those people who are so insistent on dictating the terms of our human existence? I leave you to draw your own conclusions.

As for the idea of mediums putting plants in their audiences, this is both ridiculous and preposterous and, quite frankly, it simply could not be done. Consider this... A medium will hold five demonstrations in the course of an average week. As a rule, he will forge a dozen links over the course of a two and a half hour demonstration. So, being conservative about it and allowing for bank holidays, Easter and Christmas, say he delivers forty messages in any one week. This means he would have to have forty people in his employ who follow him round to every demonstration he puts on. How long do you think he could do that before someone rumbled him? How long could he do that, paying forty people a weekly wage, before he went bankrupt?

People see two hundred heads crammed into a venue, they look at the price of admission and assume that either the clairvoyant or his promoter is making a fortune. Believe me, and I speak as one who promoted a clairvoyant for more than 10 years, nothing could be further from the truth. After you take into consideration the price of the advertising, the hire charge for the venue, the price of the petrol, the taxman's percentage, the cost of printing and postage, there is seldom an awful lot left and I can remember more than one incident when, at the end of the evening I've been embarrassed to put £20 in my client's hand saying "sorry mate, but that's your fee for the night!" Not enough here to pay for a taxi home, never mind the wages for forty stooges!

In Sandy's case the idea is even more ludicrous. Say she attends three demonstrations in every week and at each demonstration she produces six different pictures... Do you really think she has managed to coerce 18 people into describing or providing a photograph of a departed loved one? 18 people a week is 74 people per month which is over 800 people a year. Consider the time and effort it would take to arrange such a routine. Frankly, it would be impossible - there are only so many hours in every day. After their demonstrations most mediums are left tired, drained and exhausted. In Sandy's case family commitments make demands on her limited leisure time during the course of the day.

In the same way that a medium may not know who a message is for until it is claimed by a member of the audience, Sandy has no idea who she is sketching until the picture is identified and claimed.

Now, having said what I have just said, it grieves me to admit that there *are* a few fraudulent mediums practicing in Britain today and on more than one occasion I have been tempted to report them to both the police and the Trading Standards Association. These few rotten apples know exactly who they are *(and they know that I know who they are)* and in my opinion they are despicable in their manipulation of the vulnerable and the bereaved. This is the worst kind of criminality and in my opinion the perpetrators should be locked up for a very long time. However, to say that every medium is a fraud would be the same as saying that every priest is a paedophile. It simply isn't true and the vast majority of mediums and priests work hard at their calling with dedication and honour.

Eight: Visual Evidence

Sandy's first contact with the medium Stephen Holbrook was an auspicious meeting. True to his promise he duly contacted her six weeks or so after they'd first met in Scarborough, and this led to Sandy accompanying Stephen on several of his demonstrations. She would sit quietly by the corner of the stage or platform sketching away while he brought messages through to members of the audience. Although it didn't happen immediately, a natural symbiosis took place and invariably she found herself drawing the faces of the spirit people he was linking with – this latter fact confirmed time and again by people who'd received a message who then went to see what Sandy had produced. Stephen says that it was as if his guide and Sandy's guide had got together on the other side and were working in harmony. It's interesting to note that as Sandy's new found talent began to develop, a new guide had stepped in to dictate the direction of her art work. Sandy is, and always has been, quite adamant that it is not she who is doing the drawing, but the spirit guide who works through her hand.

Sometimes there was some confusion, especially when the guide pushed her into using both hands at the same time to draw two different portraits… This caused Sandy to feel very disorientated and dizzy and she had to insist on a compromise. She would let the spirit use both hands on condition that they were drawing a portrait of the same person. Even then, it took some time to settle in to the regime, further confusion being caused by virtue of the fact that Sandy's sketches would often be in reverse profile and usually, if she was drawing a mature adult or elderly person, the art work would depict the subject as being significantly younger than they were at the point of death.

After working with this medium for a number of months, heir respective spirit guides refined a procedure whereby Stephen could touch one of Sandy's portraits and then go immediately to the person in the audience that it connected with. By Stephen's own admission this made his task much easier, and easier still when Sandy started using an overhead projection screen so hat the audience could see what she was drawing while she was n the process of drawing it.

When, a few weeks ago, I talked to Sandy about some of he pictures she might like to include in this book she looked a little bemused.

"James, it's going to be difficult to choose. I've got so many sketches and letters that people have sent me, I wouldn't know where to begin! Can't you have a look and just pick the ones you think are the best?"

Well, yes, I *could* have done that, but Sandy was right when she said there were a lot to choose from and I was aware that with a book of this size one could only include so many illustrations. The professional thing to have done was to have followed Sandy's suggestion and spent some time cherry picking a dozen of the best examples of her work, but instead I just gathered up a random bundle of files. Doing it this way, no one could accuse me of favouritism or selectivity and I figured that in employing this tactic it would allow the world of spirit to have some say as to who and what went into the book.

Sandy's method of filing is fairly straight forward. She keeps a photocopied version of the picture she had drawn, along with any correspondence and photographs subsequently received from the recipient of the original picture. Also, when she has them, she adds a brief account of the circumstances and back story.

For example, let's look at the case of Gary Davies of Pontefract who desperately wanted a portrait of his Mother, Renee.

Renee Davies

Renee Davies had been an actress and a singer travelling all over the world to various theatres and film sets. She did a good job in passing her genes on to her son, for Gary is also a professional musician.

There was an initial problem inasmuch that Gary had hurt his hand and couldn't write – and Sandy, when she is commissioned to do a portrait, takes much of the energy from the client's handwriting. Sandy asked Gary to scribble roughly over the back of the request form and hoped that this would be enough to give her the psychic impetus to do a half decent job. You may judge for yourself on the next pages. Needless to say -- but I'm going to say it anyway in a very loud voice – Sandy was not given any verbal description of Renee by her son, Gary, and she only the saw the photographs when Gary sent them to her *after* he had received the portrait.

Renee Davies

Kath Morrison

Sandy has a lovely letter from a lady called Glenda Mc-Glone of Hull who attended one of Stephen Holbrook's evenings of clairvoyance. The last message of the evening was, in fact, for Glenda's daughter and while Stephen was delivering it, Sandy sat in her corner of the room quietly sketching away. When Glenda went over to see what Sandy had done she was stunned to see a detailed portrait of her late mother, Mrs Kath Morrison, who had very recently passed over aged 77 years.

When Glenda got home she made herself a cup of tea and found herself looking at the funeral acknowledgment sheet that was still laid out on the kitchen table. She felt that Sandy's picture represented a very true likeness – even down to the necklace worn around her mother's neck. Sandy points out that this picture is a very good example of spirits presenting themselves as being significantly younger than they were at the time of their passing.

Kath Morrison

Molly Hurditch

Molly Hurditch passed over at only 17 years old but her story is testimony to the determination of spirit to make contact with those loved ones left behind, even if they have to do it in a very circuitous way.

Sandy provides the background for Molly's story. "On Stephen's evening of clairvoyance at the Retford demonstration he made contact with Molly, who appeared to him to be either deaf or mentally compromised. I drew her face but sadly no one knew who she was. I hung on to the drawing because I knew that sooner or later she would find her way home to the right person.

"A couple of nights later in Sheffield I was instructed by Spirit to place Molly's picture on the bottom of my easel so that the audience could see her. At the end of the evening a lady approached me and asked me if Molly's picture had been claimed by anyone – and as I looked into her eyes I felt the familiar tingle as Spirit moved in close to me. I heard Molly's voice exclaim "Mum!" and I told the lady that I was certain that this picture was for her. I was surrounded by crowds of people and really couldn't talk properly but we had a long chat the following day.

"As soon as Molly's Mum phoned I felt Molly come very close to me. She wanted me to tell her mother that she was fine and had been met on the other side by her sister, Amy. It was clear that Molly did have some severe learning difficulties but she knew that the word RETFORD was very important... And you'll remember that she first came through a few days earlier when we were in Retford. Anyway, it turns out that Molly's family's address was *Retford Road*, albeit in Sheffield, and she'd grabbed at the very first opportunity to make contact.

"The most absolutely wonderful part of the story is that in talking to Molly there was no sign of any mental disability, but it's kind of curious that I've drawn her as she was when she was seven years old rather than at 17, which was the age she was

87

when she died. But then again, as I understand it, she only had a mental age of about seven…"

Adding to Sandy's notes we have a different perspective provided by Molly's mother, Jayne Hurditch. She wrote Sandy a detailed letter and I have her permission to reproduce it in full. Here's her version of events as they unfolded at Sheffield's Royal Victoria Hotel.

"I attended the session with my friends, Jo and Lesley. We went along and sat near the middle. Stephen came out and started relaying messages while Sandy drew peoples' faces. I was hoping to get a message but nothing came in the first half. During the interval we talked to people who did get messages and thought how lucky they were. In the second half I thought that Stephen was coming to me but it was the lady directly behind me who had a message from her sister. As the evening drew to a close we noticed a picture of a young girl up on Sandy's board and commented that Stephen hadn't mentioned her.

"Lesley said that she looked a bit like my daughter Molly when she was younger, so we went up to the front and asked Sandy who the little girl was. Sandy said, 'You know her, don't you!' and I told her that I thought it might be my daughter. Sandy said this little girl had first come through in Retford on May 24th but no one at that session had claimed her. Both Stephen and Sandy said how insistent she was that she found her family.

"I was absolutely stunned by this. My daughter had died on the 12th of May and her funeral had been on May 24th. We don't live in Retford but we do live on Retford Road in Sheffield. Stephen then said that this little girl was not 'perfect' in this world and that she had difficulty hearing and understanding. I told them that Molly was a girl with special needs and had difficulty understanding things. It's my firm belief that she knew she had to come through and speak to Stephen and got mixed up with Retford and Retford Road.

Molly Hurditch

"I spoke to Sandy the next day and she went on to tell me that Molly was happy and healthy and was being looked after by my Nan and Grandad. She also said that her sister, Amy, who passed away in 1999 had been there when she'd died and had looked after her. I can't tell you how much comfort I got from that. I hoped that they would have found each other and been okay. My two beautiful girls!

"My life will never be the same again. I have no children now. I think, in time, when things aren't so raw, I'll be able to think about them being together, somewhere close to me and that one day I will definitely see them again, and that belief makes me think that just possibly I might be able to get on with my life. Thank you, Sandy and Stephen, so much…

Jayne Hurditch."

89

Dean Clark

There is a curious consistency in the workings of spirit. Sometimes, just to emphasize a point, there is a double link... a second message offered to confirm the validity of the first. Such is the case in the story of Dean Clark and the best way of telling this story is to reproduce the letter that Sandy received from Dean's parents, Avril and Graham Clark, of Chesterfield.

"Dear Sandy – we spoke to you in Blackpool on April 21st at an evening of clairvoyance with Stephen Holbrook and we promised to write to you.

"The first time we saw you was when you were in Chesterfield back in 2009. We were so amazed by your portraits that we asked you to do one for us by post. The drawing that we received a couple of weeks later reminded us so much of our son Dean who died on October 1st 2007. He was only 34 and passed over with a brain tumour.

"After his death we had a photograph of him enlarged and framed which had been taken when he was 21 years old. The drawing that you did had the same likeness as the photograph!

"This is not the end of the story because two years later we saw you again with Stephen Holbrook, and on that evening we had a contact with our son. You did another portrait of him that was almost an exact copy of the first drawing you did for us.

"We are amazed at your talent and would like to thank you for the comfort you have given us.

"Yours sincerely – Avril and Graham Clark"

I think that one of the key points here is that after a two-year gap Sandy can produce two almost identical portraits. Two years is a long time in the life of a busy medium, constantly bombarded by the demands of spirit and public alike. One could not reasonably expect Sandy to remember a drawing she had done 24 months earlier (or even the people she had done it for) to the extent that she was able to reproduce it, almost line for line!

Dean Clark

Andy Baker and AJ

Sandy received a phone call from a young man called Andy wanting to know what he had to do to get a portrait done. Sandy, who really has no idea who she's going to be drawing, promised to send him one in the post. When Andy received the picture he phoned Sandy to say how amazed he was to find he was looking at a portrait – of himself!

While talking to him Sandy became aware of a gentleman in spirit who, she felt sure, was Andy's father. The gentleman was holding the hand of a little boy whose name, he said, was "J". (Actually the child's name was "AJ" but he was universally known as just "J".) As soon as the telephone conversation was over Sandy found herself furiously sketching the image of the little boy, which she subsequently sent off to Andy.

Andy's father had very recently passed over and the family were still struggling with the loss. A few weeks later little AJ had seen his Daddy's van pull into the road and had run out of the house to meet him. Andy didn't see the child and AJ ran under the wheels of his father's vehicle and was killed. Sandy received this information through her contact with Andy's father in spirit but she did not know that it was Andy's van that had killed the boy until Andy told her this later. One cannot imagine the emotions experienced by little AJ's family and, in particular, by his father. Andy confessed to Sandy that he had received a great deal of comfort from his contact with his father and son and knowing that they were together made this double tragedy just a little easier to bear.

Andy

"AJ"

The Case of John Knight

As I've said, when Sandy sits down to do a drawing she really has no idea of what (or who) the result will be. This is why she always suggests that people who do not immediately recognise the portrait should do some research and the connection is usually found eventually. And so it was in the case of John Knight.

Mrs. Brenda Knight asked Sandy to do a portrait for her but when the picture arrived she really had no idea who it was. She checked through the usual pile of family snaps but nobody faintly resembled the young man Sandy had depicted. Brenda almost forgot about the whole business until a good while later she was going through some old belongings of her late husband that she'd kept stuffed away in the attic (the belongings, not her hus-

93

band) and she came upon a rather battered tin box. On opening the box she found a little hoard of memorabilia from World War II including a dog eared ration book and an even more dog eared photograph of a handsome young man in uniform. She immediately identified him as being her late husband's older brother (someone she'd never met) and after some genealogical research learned that he had been shot down in a Beaufort bomber returning from a raid on Norway in 1942.

I suppose the moral of this story is if you're among the small percentage of people who don't immediately recognise Sandy's drawings, it always pays to do a bit of research.

John Knight

Angela Dunn

Angela first came to Sandy's attention during a demonstration in Hull. Sandy recalls – "Angela had cervical cancer and was literally in the last couple of weeks of her life. She came out of the hospice just to attend the demonstration, hoping that she would have contact with her Grandad and her small son, Shane. She was so desperate to have final proof of life after death that her mother asked Stephen if he might have a quiet word with her during the interval. Stephen did this willingly and said that although obviously he couldn't promise anything, he hoped there might be a contact during the second half of the evening. As the second half began, I resolved to have a word with the young lady myself. Maybe you don't need much reassurance when death is a lifetime away but when you know it's just around the corner you tend to feel a bit differently about it.

"The second half of the evening began and Angela's Grandad did come through, bringing with him the little boy called, Shane. Stephen gave some very evidential messages from the Grandfather, whose name I think was Charles, and while he was doing it I managed to draw a portrait of the little boy, complete with the very clothing he was buried in and some of the little things that had been placed on his grave.

"Soon after that evening in Hull, Angela's Mum, Karen, had a telephone reading with me. By this time Angela had passed into spirit, but she came back to be reunited with her mother and her eldest daughter.

"Nine weeks later the whole family came out to another of Stephen's evenings at which time Angela came through to Stephen with some fantastic evidence and that was when I was able to draw the portrait of Angela. Her mother was delighted and felt that she could not have asked for more."

And now, to get a different slant on the same story, here is Karen Dunn's memoir of recollections, reproduced unedited.

95

"My daughter, Angela, was terminally ill with cervical cancer when we went to see Stephen Holbrook and Sandy Ingham the last time they came to Hull. We'd seen them both before and thought their talents were amazing.

Angela

"Angela was so ill and we knew her time was running out but she was desperate to see Stephen again so we all went along together and I'll never forget what happened that night.

"There was me, my two daughters, my daughter's partner, my mother, my friend and my sister. We all prayed that Angela would get a message – and she did! Angela lost a baby boy in March 1999 and he came through with Angela's Grandad who told her that he'd been looking after baby Shane and that they were both waiting for her on the other side.

"When we looked at the portrait that Sandy had drawn, we couldn't believe it. She'd drawn baby Shane and she'd even drawn what he was buried in. Not only that, she'd drawn a Teddy and a few toys that we'd put on Shane's grave.

"Stephen came across and talked to us and he said he thought I was more scared than my daughter – which was probably true – and then he told Angela that she would go to sleep one night and wake up in a beautiful place! This gave us so much comfort, especially Angela, because even though she had been so brave she knew she was going to die. Two weeks later she passed away.

"My eldest Granddaughter, Laurie, kept asking if we could go to Stephen's next demonstration because Angela had promised her that she would come through to us with a message, just to let us know that she was okay. So we went along, but I really didn't think we would get a message. Some people go for years without getting one, but Laurie was quite convinced that we would and we were all gobsmacked when we *did*!

"She'd only been gone for nine weeks but she came through loud and clear, saying that her funeral had been lovely – because we were all worried that it had all gone wrong because the priest who took the service was Angela's auntie who had senile dementia and on the day she forgot some of the Lord's Prayer. We all said that Angela would have laughed but actually I was quite upset that it hadn't gone to plan.

"I'm telling you this because she made a joke about it, mentioning the name of Josie, which was the name of Angela's auntie, and she also wanted to reassure me that the wine was free in heaven which was a private joke between me and Angela, because I like my wine… She also thanked me for sticking to my promise to take care of her seven children because it was her worst fear that they would be split up.

"We cannot say how much all this means to us. It has changed our lives. I have always believed in an afterlife but having the proof that Angela and Shane are okay means everything."

Suzanne Bilton's Evidence

"Dear Sandy – thank you for the beautiful picture, it meant so much... Since my father passed away in July 2010 after an 18 month battle with terminal lung cancer, I've wanted just that extra proof that the spirit world exists. So, in November 2010 it was the first demonstration locally that you were doing. Me, my sister and my friend went hoping and praying that he would come through. Leaving that night I was really disappointed that I didn't get a reading but decided that in February 2011 we would try again. Me and my friend travelled to Sheffield. Again, an enjoyable night, but nothing. I thought that maybe it just wasn't my turn. By chance I realized that there was a demonstration a week later in Chesterfield and I felt the need to go to this one. We went but after the last two times I wasn't getting my hopes up. After the first couple of readings I thought that this was going to be another night with nothing. It was coming to the interval and Stephen says that his guide was telling him he had to wait but he didn't know why. At the same time you were doing your portraits as normal. Stephen was still being told to wait by his guide, so he told us a story of something that happened the night before. Then he started by asking if anyone had lost a baby on the back row. Me and my friend were on the back row with a few others, but no-one was putting their hand up. Nervously, I raised my hand and said I hadn't lost a baby but my brother was a baby when he passed. My heart was pounding because it was me that he wanted to speak to.

"My Nanna also came through and everything Stephen was saying was spot on. Half way through the reading he turned around to look at the portrait you were doing and he stopped in amazement. There was not one, not two but three portraits on the page. It had never been done before and he was so excited he took the portrait half way through to show everybody then gave it you back to finish.

"After the emotional reading there was still no mention of my father but when I went to collect the picture there on the page clear as day staring back at me was my dad, as well as a woman and a baby. I wasn't too sure who they were as my brother had passed away before I was born. I couldn't wait to visit my mum to show her and find out who they were.

"The next morning I showed my mum and she says that the baby resembles my sister as a baby and a bit of my brother that had passed. We couldn't think of who the other woman was but I told my mum to sort out some old photos as I had to copy them and post to you so you could put them in your book. After a while she came down with the photos with one in particular. It was a picture of my mum in her 30s. It was shocking, the resemblance, even the hairstyle was the same. So the picture was my mum (in her 30s) still living, dad in spirit looking as he did just before he passed and baby.

Suzanne's Father

Suzanne's Mother in her 30's

"The picture has really helped knowing that they are still with us, watching and looking after us. I'm framing the picture and it will take pride of place in my house...

Many thanks...Suzanne"

Julie's Evidence

"I lost my beautiful daughter five years ago in 2005. She was 21 and studying at a flight school in Florida to become a commercial pilot. Ten weeks into her course, whilst flying a plane solo, she lost her life when the plane crashed. We later found out the plane had a faulty flap switch and because of this I lost my daughter.

"I began looking for answers and for me I felt the need to find a medium who could reach her and give me proof that one day I will be with her again. I was an atheist and now I would say that I'm an agnostic. I have seen about 30 different mediums from wacky to bad and to average.

"I had never heard of Sandy Ingham and had never been to see Stephen Holbrook before. But in July 2010 as I read my local paper I noted that he was coming to town very soon and seeing that a psychic artist was performing with him made me want to book.

"His performance was stunning, entertaining and very emotional but Sandy's talent is amazing. How can she draw not just one portrait but two together in five minutes. Wow!

"I filled in a form for a portrait to be done and handed the money over to a man – he told me he couldn't take hold of the form, his wife Sandy had to touch it herself. Then in the interval my mum who was with me decided she wanted to order one too, so I escorted her to the front of the hall to pay for hers.

"As mum was waiting to pay, Sandy came straight up to me and looked into my eyes and just came out with "who's Lisa?"

"After five years of searching for the right medium, to say I was shocked is such an understatement. I was frozen to the spot, gob smacked and frightened. I never thought this would ever happen. I grabbed mum's hand to come and listen. Sandy said she had my dad with her and that Lisa wanted to give me a hug. We both found our seats and sat in stunned silence for the second part of the show.

"Two weeks later our portraits arrived. Both were male pictures. We were gutted as we had so hoped it would be Lisa. Mine was a picture of my uncle who had passed away about seven years earlier. I needed to make an appointment for a one to one reading with Sandy, but just something was stopping me from doing this. I was so frightened of what I would hear, I just could not ring her.

"Four months later, and only because I was moving further away from where she lived, I decided to ring her. The date was fixed for Sunday 28th November 2010.

"This next bit might seem like the most boring information about my car, but just remember it as it just might give you goose bumps later.

"We had just had our 4x4 car in for a service and been told that the bearing had gone on the back and it was advisable not to drive the car in case it seized up completely – but I was determined to make that appointment. We begged our neighbour to lend us her car (not a 4x4) but when we woke up on that morning the weather was atrocious, another foot of snow had fallen during the night and the forecast was for more snow during the day. But still I was determined to get there. We made it just, but had to park the car on the main road about 80 metres away from Sandy's house as her road was just too bad to take an ordinary car along – especially as it wasn't ours.

"We were both welcomed and warmed up with a cup of tea and my reading began. Sandy explained how she worked, told us a bit about her life and then, boom, she came straight out with 'What happened to your car? Where is the blue one?'

"Wow – who could have known that – only our kind neighbour who had lent us her black car, while our blue car sat on our drive! And that was just the start. Three hours and fifty minutes later we said our goodbyes and carefully drove home stunned.

"I had been in touch with my daughter – the first time in five years – it was like the telephone call I have missed and wished for all the time since she died. Sandy even got in exquisite detail the exact fault on the plane, which could only be found when the micro switch from the wreckage was sent off by NTSB (National Transport Safety Board) flight inspectors to be examined by experts in microscopic forensics in New York.

"The content of the reading contained details that only myself and Lisa would have known. There is no explanation! Other than 100% proof that Lisa passed this on to Sandy, who relayed it on to me.

"It's been a long, hard, sad five years and each day is just another day that I live without her. Oh how I wish I could have a connection with her every day. I miss the trivia a mother and daughter talk about. I miss her love, cuddles and her smell, but at least I now know that one day I will be with her again and this is the belief Sandy has given me. Bless you, Sandy, I can now live for that day.

Lisa at 16 and 21 (taken 2 days before she died)

"If that isn't proof enough, I will share the portrait Sandy did for me that day with you. Sandy said she would try to draw a portrait for us, but not to get our hopes up as sometimes you don't get the one you want (as we already knew). She started drawing and as soon as she started pencilling long hair I just knew it was Lisa. The portrait is amazing and she couldn't have done better if Lisa was standing in front of her – but as we know, Lisa was!

"Julie."

Lisa

Brenda Waker

Brenda was one of those slightly larger than life character ladies that you often see on some of the TV soaps and who frequently crop up as a protagonist in some of the social novels of the 60s and 70s. She was an East London girl who worked hard and played hard and who most assuredly had no interest in spiritualism and who did not believe in life after death...

And yet, most curiously, about six months prior to her passing, Brenda suddenly expressed an interest in the subject and started accompanying her daughter, Carly, to various spiritualist meetings and demonstrations of clairvoyance. One might assume that she'd experienced some health problem that caused her to consider her own mortality or had some inkling that something was wrong and that there might be trouble ahead, but when one considers that she died without warning with a sudden brain haemorrhage – on Christmas Eve of all days – then this premise seems unlikely.

When Carly saw that a medium was coming to her home town of Bury St. Edmunds, she immediately booked a ticket and was surprised and delighted to receive a message of love and reassurance from her mother.

Brenda

Uncle Rowley

After seeing Sandy in Driffield, Mrs Lynn Hunter asked if she would do a portrait for her, and she picks up the story from there…

"What a surprise I got when the portrait arrived and I saw that it was my Uncle Rowley. Sadly, he passed away with cancer a few years ago and the last time I saw him, just before he died, he was very thin and this upset me very much. I think the portrait is his way of saying 'look, I'm back to how I used to be and don't be upset anymore.'

"Also, the week I sent off for the portrait it was my birthday. Every year my uncle would send me a card and put a letter in

Uncle Rowley

105

with it even though he only lived a few miles away. I think that Sandy's portrait was my birthday card from him.

"Sandy had also mentioned that someone had been shouting the name 'Harry' at her. After some thought I realized that it wasn't Harry but 'Marrie.' Marrie was Rowley's sister who used to come with me to the nursing home when he was poorly.

"It's lovely to know that Uncle Rowley is now back to being his old self. I can't thank Sandy enough for the portrait. I was actually hoping that my Dad would have come through to have his portrait done but Sandy told me that he didn't like having his picture done, not even in a photograph, which is true because he didn't. Maybe, one day he'll change his mind.

Love from Lynn Hunter"

Pippa Chester

First of all let me quote from Sandy's notes. She says:- "This was a first for me. Nicky Chester desperately wanted to know that her baby girl, Pippa, was safe in the world of spirit., I sent Nicky a sketch which led to her telling me that she would love to know what Pippa looked like now. Pippa was a twin and by then would have been about four years old. I asked my artist guide and the portrait was duly drawn. I think it shows an uncanny resemblance to Pippa's twin brother, Rowan, and her younger brother, Finn."

I have four letters that Nicky sent Sandy, and one section in the last letter seems particularly relevant: "I enclose a whole load of photographs of the two boys. Rowan is very difficult to photograph, especially smiling. Actually, I see more of Pippa in his younger brother, Finn, who is a smiley bright and bouncy boy, and I suppose that's how I imagine Pippa to be. Sometimes I look at Finn and just for a fleeting second I think I'm looking at Pippa. I don't get this with Rowan but there is a huge family resemblance between the portrait and both my sons.

Rowan

Finn

This story raises the issue of what happens to young children and babies when they pass over. Do they remain babies and children forever or is there some form of celestial aging process? Usually, if a baby is making a link with a parent through a clairvoyant medium, an older spirit, sometimes in the form of a departed grandparent or similar, will bring the baby through and speak on its behalf. For example, Nicky Chester was able to identify her baby as a baby but would she have recognised her as a four year old? (Actually, she did, but only with the help of Sandy's portrait!) Assume though that a parent loses a child of 10, and 15 years later that child comes through as a 25 year old... There would inevitably be some problem with the process of recognition, so although the child may have grown in the spirit world, for the purposes of identification it will present itself in a recognisable form, i.e. the age that it was when it passed over.

I understand that if you're a grumpy old bugger over here, then you'll be a grumpy old bugger over there – but only for the purpose of recognition with people left behind on the earth plane. In the spirit world, if time exists at all, you can be sure it exists in a very different way than it does down here.

This concept of timelessness in spirit can be difficult to grasp and, to tell you the truth, I don't think that any human being can tell us *exactly* how it works. Even the measurement of time down here on the earth plane is an example of Man's arrogance, for time is not an absolute that can be measured accurately by science. There are minutes within hours, and hours within days. There are days within weeks and weeks within years. There are years within lifetimes. Day follows night and summer follows spring, but as anyone who is truly in tune with Spirit will tell you, there are *not* always 24 hours in a day, there are *not* always seven days in a week, and there are *not* always 52 weeks in a year. From all I have learned, read and have been told by people who know far more than me, I think this must be a reflection of what it is like, albeit on a much grander scale, in the world of spirit.

As I say, time is not a universal absolute to be measured by the passing of nanoseconds within the mechanism of some fancy nuclear clock. It is subjective to the person living through and experiencing their own time. Does five minutes in the dentist's chair having root canal work last as long as five minutes having the most glorious sex with the love of your life? Does the second week of your holiday seem to last as long as the first week, or does it fly past at twice the speed? If you live for 70 years, do the last 10 years seem as long as those never ending summers of your childhood or are they suddenly gone in little more than a blink of an eye? How long is one year for the prisoner in his cell? Is it as long, shorter or longer than the free soul who spends the same year dancing and laughing and popping champagne corks at every opportunity?

So, if time is subjective to the individual on the earth plane consider for a moment just how much more complicated the concept might be in the world of spirit where there is no measurement of time – at least, not as we know it, subjective or otherwise! The lady who waits for 10 years to get a message from her deceased husband has much in common with the gentleman who gets a message from his Mother who passed away within the past week insofar that as far as the two spirits are concerned, they very possibly have waited the same length of time.

I offer these words as an overview of spiritual belief – a reflection of perceived wisdom – but I cannot give you an iron clad guarantee that it's absolutely right. It sounds right and it *feels* right and for the want of anything better I am prepared to accept it at its face value.

Whilst not in the least bit evangelical, Sandy is 100% committed to her belief and conviction. She has been a medium all of her life and has the benefit of a lifetime's worth of evidence. She does not welcome death but has no fear of dying and through her drawings she seeks to provide evidence for an afterlife and, as such, remove much of the fear associated with death.

Why, she asks, should one fear death when it's just a gateway to life everlasting?

Nine: Altered States

For anyone who claims there is no evidence of life after death they should look in Sandy's filing cabinet. There they will find a veritable mountain of evidence in the form of drawings, photographs and unsolicited testimonials. As I say, when it came to choosing some examples of her work to go in the book, I just picked up the nearest bundle and then spent the next couple of weeks wading through it and, without editing the content, placing it in some kind of chronological order to coincide with the page count.

There was one file that caught my attention and caused a tremendous degree of excitement. This was the story of Harold Hancock, an old soldier who succeeded in getting a vital message through to his family. The key thing is that Harold wasn't dead! The implications of this event are highly significant in a number of different ways, but first let's pick up on Harold's story as told to Sandy by Harold's niece, Mrs Rita Tempest, of Knaresborough.

She writes: "Dear Sandy, thank you for the portrait you sent me which has just arrived. I thought you would like to know who the soldier is. This is my uncle, Harold Hancock, my late aunt's husband. What is amazing is that Uncle Harold is still alive!

"He has been resident in a home for the last two years ever since he had a severe stroke. He is not able to communicate as his speech is impaired and he gets so frustrated when he cannot talk to people. He recognises me, I think, and I often wonder if he knows what I'm saying to him and what he'd want to say to me if only he could. Although to all intents and purposes he's simply no longer with us, there must be some part of his brain that is still working.

"I know that if he was able to tell me, he wouldn't be happy in the state he's in now and wouldn't want to carry on living as he is living, but despite his condition he's still found some way to communicate with his family and that is amazing."

Sandy has had some correspondence with Rita and is able to fill in some of the details. Initially, when she had completed the portrait, she scribbled a few lines of a message that she'd picked up while doing the sketch. She told Rita that "the gentleman in the picture says please keep talking to me because I do hear you!"

Harold Hancock

This was a very important message as Rita had felt that her visits were a waste of time because seemingly she wasn't getting through to her uncle on any level, and therefore she had decided not to visit so often. Sandy's message changed all that, and now she continues to visit regularly, secure in the knowledge that even if her old soldier of an uncle isn't in a position to have a normal conversation, he is hearing what Rita has to say. Indeed, as absolute proof of this, when Rita had shown her uncle the picture Sandy had drawn and had asked him if he knew who it was, he replied quite clearly "It's me!"

This gave Rita and the nursing staff quite a jolt because these were Harold's first and only words since having the stroke.

Now, Harold Hancock was not dead. He wasn't even in a coma, but as a result of the stroke and encroaching old age he had lapsed into an ever deepening state of catatonia where his mind was literally out of his head. In this state of isolation, he was unable to communicate either with his relatives or the nursing staff of the care home in which he was resident – but somehow he had managed to reach through the ether to make contact with Sandy and was able to pass on that most important message... *I can hear you so please keep coming to visit and please keep talking to me!*

If Harold was able to achieve this from his catatonic state, when, for want of a better expression, his mind was detached from the rest of his body, it encourages a more subtle question... Are the rest of us, when *our* minds are out of *our* bodies, say perhaps when we are dreaming, also able to communicate without words or physical contact, with our friends and loved ones, both on this side of the grave and the other. Indeed, is there anyone we could *not* communicate with if we really set our minds to it?

This is a multi-faceted question that has to be dealt with by degree. On the latter point there is ample evidence of people being able to communicate (sometimes over ridiculously long distances) in a state of telepathic trance and I refer you to the Aboriginal traditions of Australia and the deep trance techniques as practised by the Buddhist monks of Tibet.

In our western society our minds tend only to leave our bodies when we dream – and even then there is always a strong ethereal link that holds our wandering minds in check, otherwise we'd all end up like Harold Hancock by the end of the week. Of course, there are two kinds of dream; one which occurs naturally at night while we sleep, the other being a self-induced state of altered awareness caused by meditation or medication.

Of the former – natural dream patterns that occur while we are asleep – there are sub-divisions and Sandy sums it up nicely when she says:- "First of all there are what I call 'filing cabinet' dreams. These are the dreams we experience that file away all the knowledge and snippets of information we've picked up over the day. The useful stuff that we might need later on gets shoved into one file while the rubbish that needs to be dumped and jettisoned gets put in another one. Some people say they never dream, but everyone has these filing cabinet dreams and it's just that a lot of people don't remember them. Those of us who do remember tend to remember disjointed snippets, which is why dreams always seem so jumbled and muddled. In one dream you could be playing tennis with Andy Murray, in another dream you're sailing on a cruise ship around the Isle of Wight and in a third dream maybe you're in a cinema watching Humphrey Bogart and Ingrid Bergman in Casablanca. When you wake up you remember a dream where you've been playing tennis on a cruise ship with Humphrey Bogart and Ingrid Bergman. All the snippets roll into one to create a confused and very mismatched memory.

"Then there's what I call the prophetic dream. This is when you "see" something in your dream state that you couldn't possibly see with your own eyes while you were awake. This needn't be anything dramatic. If, for example, in one of your dreams you see an old friend that you haven't thought about let alone seen for half a dozen years, don't be surprised if either there's an accidental meeting or out of the blue that person gets in touch with you. If you see your Mum, who might live at the other end of the country, buying a new red coat, well don't be surprised if you subsequently learn that your Mum's bought a new red coat!

"Sometimes you *do* dream of major events. Someone I knew dreamt he was drowning on a sinking ship. He was sup-

113

posed to travel to Holland by ferry the following day but he was so disturbed by the dream that he paid the extra money and went by plane instead… And that was the day of the Zebrugge ferry disaster! Of course, from a dreamer's point of view it's all very confusing because you can't always tell the difference between a prophetic dream and a filing cabinet dream – at least, not while you're having it, you can't! You've got to wait for the prophesy to come true before you can realize that you've had a prophetic dream and by then most people have moved on in their busy lives and it no longer seems important or has quite the same impact.

"Finally, there are visitational dreams in which we are visited by spirits and we venture the first few footsteps into the world of spirit to meet with loved ones who have passed over. It's two way traffic! I'd be the first to acknowledge that not everyone has this kind of dream but I think I can safely say that when we do have one, we know about it, because it always leaves a strong residual memory. It is in these dreams that I believe we are able to have communication with our loved ones who have passed over and although I can't prove it for certain, I think that these dreams are initiated by our loved ones and that they come to us in these special dreams to bring us support and comfort and whatever guidance and encouragement they can give."

Of course, when we are asleep, and whether we are dreaming or not, we are in some kind of altered state – something other than our everyday consciousness. But there are, of course, other "altered states" such as the level of awareness that is attained by the spiritualist medium when they enter a trance as a precursor to making contact with someone from the spirit world. Sandy might not go into the kind of trance you frequently see portrayed on TV and in the movies, but without any doubt, while Leo is working through her and she is doing her drawings, her mind is somewhere else other than in the room with two hundred people and, furthermore, it is so far gone into that "somewhere else" that she loses all contact with her real world surroundings.

It is when mediums and psychics are in this state that they are unfettered by the normal restraints of consciousness and their minds become more receptive to the subtle vibrations of awareness that are obfuscated and drowned out by the distractions and the clamour of the human condition.

This is not mystical mumbo jumbo but medical fact based on a plethora of research that has been going on, albeit somewhat sporadically, ever since the 1930s. Indeed, there was a high point of interest in the 60s through to the late 70s when the American military was experimenting with mind enhancing drugs, such as LSD, and the Soviets were spending billions of rubles every year on research into telepathy and mind control. The Americans tried talking to Dolphins and the Russians were trying to talk to their cosmonauts in orbit around the moon: neither side faired very well, but what is interesting is that for many long and expensive years, they tried!

Despite all these ruminations we must not lose sight of the fact that Harold Hancock reached out through his catatonia and made a *spiritual* contact with the searching mind of Sandy's mediumship.

If nothing else this should give us good cause to review our terms of reference when we speak of such conditions and review the possibilities even further when considering the plight of those who hover between life and death in the state of coma. While neither Sandy nor I can see the day when the medical fraternity might open their arms in welcome, just imagine the possibilities…

What if a person who had been in a deep coma for weeks or months or even years could be contacted by a medium and through that contact could make their wishes known? More importantly, *what if* that same person who had been locked into a coma for so long, could have their mind coaxed back into their body by the medium and, obviously under stringent medical supervision, be brought back fully conscious into the real world? After all, if as part of their everyday lives, mediums can contact the dead, why should it be so difficult to contact the living?

Ten: Doreen, Doctors, State & Church

Despite the maternal rejection when she was a child, Sandy had a deep and abiding love for her mother – which she saw as an ongoing battle to gain her mother's attention and approval. It was only when Sandy's maternal grandmother passed into Spirit that there seemed to be a softening in her mother's demeanour and behaviour which led to the gradual establishment of a loving relationship between the two women. It might not have been a perfect union but it was far more than Sandy had ever had in the past and was far more than she'd ever hoped to get.

As the advance of old age caught up with the fleeting span of human years, Sandy's mother was diagnosed with breast cancer which rapidly spread to multiple cancers throughout her body. Doreen came to live with Sandy and Mike in Bridlington and considering that Doreen had always been terrified by the prospect of any kind of illness or injury, Sandy did a remarkably good job of creating a calm and healing atmosphere.

Sandy's sister, Elaine, still lived in Lincoln and so while Sandy was working in the area it seemed logical to take Doreen over to Elaine's for a few days' holiday. On the day she was supposed to be picked up she had a stroke and was admitted to one of Lincoln's leading hospitals.

Sandy immediately rushed to her Mother's bedside. Doreen was unconscious but later that afternoon she came around and at some time in the early evening found enough strength to put her fingers to her temple in the manner of a gun, indicating that as far as she was concerned it was all over and she was as good as dead.

Doreen had always been clear in her views and after Sandy had heard the doctors' appraisal of her mother's condition

117

and the very dark and "no hope" prognosis, she and Elaine had a very long and heart-breaking conversation. Sandy conveyed the family's wishes to the hospital; within the parameters of the law, Doreen's life was not to be preserved.

This was where Sandy heard the expression "The Liverpool Pathway" for the first time. This is a euphemism for the patient to be denied food and water with the minimum amount of necessary drugs administered to keep them alive just beneath the threshold of consciousness until the patient passes away. This was, and still is, the standard practice of allowing a patient to pass away naturally without pain, but it only works if the drugs are administered correctly, with special attention focused upon the timing of the medication. If a drug is late in being given, the patient starts regaining consciousness and is exposed to the pain of their condition. Frequently this pain can be quite excruciating.

On the Thursday of the week, Doreen was duly moved from A&E and admitted to the terminal care ward and the whole family came to say their goodbyes. With her son, Adrian, in attendance, Sandy literally moved into the hospital, which very kindly provided her with a bed in a side ward. Mike parked their motor home in the hospital car park and as Doreen hovered between life and death, the long vigil began.

Anyone who's ever been there will know this can be a most terrible time... You dread the ultimate bad news but you just wish it could be over soon to alleviate the suffering.

Sandy's sisters, Angela and Elaine, and Elaine's daughter, Sarah, were frequent visitors and Sandy took great comfort from their support. Sarah was a nurse at the hospital and indeed, in the past, Elaine had also been a nurse at the hospital. Sandy had every good reason to believe that her dying mother was in safe hands and getting the very best of care.

And now we come to the carelessness of youth and the best laid plans of mice and men.

Doreen had been in the hospital for five days and Sandy had hardly ever left her bedside. Having had some nursing training herself she was able to monitor – although not supervise – her mother's care and if on occasion some of the medication was a few minutes late she was able to have a quiet word with one of the nursing staff; the problem would be swiftly rectified with no harm done. Occasionally Sandy would pre-empt the medication by offering the nurse on duty a gentle reminder. As Sandy says quite candidly, "of course I knew there were other patients on the ward who were in a bad way and although I felt desperately sorry for them it was in a very detached kind of manner. My *own mother* was there and she was *dying.* That thought overwhelmed my mind and for a while nothing else mattered."

As the author of this book, I have to say that having had some experience of the French medical system, I can tell you that our NHS is probably the most wonderful health service in the world – but that doesn't make it perfect and there are some gaping holes in the cover of care that have got nothing to do with budgets, but have everything to do with bad management and the apathy of some of our hospital administrators.

Sandy and her mother, Doreen, fell into one of these holes.

On the Sunday, a junior and very inexperienced nurse was on duty. She looked at Doreen's medication package and felt that because there were so many drugs being administered to one patient that someone had made a mistake. Before giving the drugs, she wanted confirmation from a doctor that the prescription was valid – and until she got that validation she was not prepared to put her job on the line by taking responsibility.

Sandy, aware that the drugs were now late in being administered, went and had a quiet word with the young nurse and was told that the nurse "would deal with in it a minute". Several minutes passed, then a quarter of an hour… and Sandy again approached the nurse to be told that the matter was in hand and that it would be dealt with "in a minute".

Over the following half hour, Sandy made two more appeals for her mother's medication and on each occasion she was ignored.

At this time Elaine and Sarah arrived and, out of deference to their role in the hospital hierarchy, Sandy left them to try and deal with the problem of the delayed medication. Unfortunately they had no more luck than Sandy had, and by now Doreen was increasingly regaining consciousness and had begun to moan with pain. One must remember that she'd had no food or water since the Thursday and as well as the pain from the cancer she also had a severe chest infection. In short, she'd been two hours without her drugs and was becoming very distressed.

This was when, in her own words, Sandy completely lost her temper and demanded that something be done with immediate effect.

I wasn't there, but knowing Sandy I can imagine the volcano erupting with all the power of Mount Etna and God help anyone who got in the way of her pyroclastic cloud of anger. She'd tried the quiet, calm and reasonable approach which hadn't worked (it seldom does) but now her explosion of loud protest did bring immediate results and within a very short time there were a couple of doctors and senior hospital administrators on hand who recognised that a monumental cock-up had occurred and were full of apologies and reassurances that this kind of mistake had never happened before. The doctors looked stern and serious while the administrators looked worried.

It took the medical team almost two days to stabilize Doreen's condition but, despite their best efforts, early on the third day at 2.22 on the morning of August 27th (which was her birthday) Doreen finally slipped into death and found some peace and relief from the pain that she needn't have suffered had not a junior nurse seen fit to make decisions way above her pay grade and well outside the remit of her authority and experience.

Sandy watched her mother deteriorate and die, which quite understandably, has influenced her views on assisted suicide and euthanasia. She totally understands and accepts that euthanasia cannot become legal without the most stringent and ardent of safeguards, but believes that those safeguards could and should be put in place, even if it means that a team of half a dozen doctors and specialists consider every single case on its individual merit. Hospital staff agree with Sandy when she says that the only way that the medical authorities can stay within the letter of the law is to withhold fluid and sustenance until a patient passes away. She finds the idea of either the church or the state denying the individual's right to a dignified ending of their own life totally abhorrent and illogical.

The Hippocratic Oath is frequently quoted in defence of a doctor's duty to preserve life, but the Hippocratic Oath also dictates that it is the doctor's duty to alleviate suffering. Sandy is of the opinion that it may be time to review the interpretation of this contradictory oath and possibly, in line with our emergent new society, ignore the damned thing altogether if adherence to it strips the individual of their human right to dictate the time and method of their own departure from this mortal coil.

As you can imagine, Sandy has some passionate views on the subject. She asks – "Who can possibly condone a system of starving people to death? Nobody would if there was a humane choice! What does it say about our leaders? Our law makers? Every person I have spoken to, and I've spoken to hundreds of people, would pass a law to allow their loved ones to die with dignity, albeit with stringent conditions to protect the vulnerable. I watched my mother die and suffer, and you should see the photos of Mum taken a couple of days before the stroke! Although she was ill she was still beautiful. I took photos during the days from the stroke to her passing and you would not believe the horror of starvation, the trauma of watching someone you love dearly go through this process. Is this *really* what we would wish for our loved ones? 99.9% of the people I've put this question to are in favour of euthanasia in cases such as I've encountered with my Mother, so just *who* is controlling our lives to the extent that they can dictate the terms of our death in what can only be called an appalling and traumatic way. So much of the suffering is so unnecessary! One thing's for sure and that's if people had the choice they would die with dignity!"

Eleven: Psychic Development

Many people ask Sandy how they can develop their own psychic abilities, and Sandy will direct them to their local spiritualist church.

There is a residual image in some peoples' minds of a few desperate folk smelling of wet clothes gathered in damp little back street halls with dim lights and little cheer, and while it's true that there were a few spiritualist churches that did fit that description back in the 1950s and 60s, in this present day and age the spiritualist movement has become much more vibrant and vital. Congregations are diverse both in age and social background and over the last couple of decades the size of the congregations has almost doubled as more and more people realize that the spiritualist church has more to offer than most other religions. Instead of just saying "you must have faith" the spiritualist movement offers proof to indicate that one's faith is not misplaced.

It is true that there are a few rotten apples in every barrel and there are a few (very few!) people in the higher echelons of the spiritualist movement who seem to be there for their own self-aggrandisement and by the dictate of their own ego and sense of self-importance. Fortunately the spiritualist church is a very open organisation and because there is nowhere to hide, the bad apples are soon identified and sorted. Anyone approaching the spiritualist church, either in search of solace or on a quest for more information and insight into spiritual enlightenment, can be guaranteed a warm and courteous welcome and will be offered time and space to form their own opinions and evolve at their own speed.

Sandy thrived at the spiritualist church in Sleaford. For years she had struggled on alone, exposed to the world of spirit but without any real terms of reference. Sleaford not only provided those terms, it also brought her into close proximity with other people who felt and thought as she did, and proved to her great relief that rather than being alone she was in the company of some very nice people. Sandy was able to sit in development circles and as such she learned how to craft and control her mediumistic skills... Others would sit in the same or similar circles learning how to make contact with their own innate powers of clairvoyance and while some were able to proceed swiftly others needed much more time to make contact with that inner spark of spiritual sentience.

The point is, this is a natural process without timetables, exams or agendas and in this ambience of atmosphere the spiritual vibration is inevitably enhanced. How much progress can be made is very much down to the individual but everyone has *some* clairvoyant ability locked away inside. It is something we are all born with, which is why children in particular can be prone to psychic experiences. The trouble is, as we grow older and learn to deal with the all-important matters of schools, lessons, exams, homework, boyfriends, girlfriends, education et al, that natural psychic energy is squeezed out of us like juice from an apple in a cider press. We have so much other stuff in our head that there simply isn't room for it – we lose it or it gets lost. But like anything that is lost, it can be found again, especially if one knows where to look.

Sandy shares my view and adds her own comments – "One of the things I always say is everyone has some psychic ability! Some people may call it intuition, that sense of 'knowing', and if they trust those feelings and allow the mind to go ahead, a picture starts to develop... The hardest thing is to trust those imaginings and to verbalize them. We all think in pictures, and sometimes we will see a face or faces that we don't recognise. We tend to accept these strange faces as random people, but they are so often a communication from Spirit, presented to us in picture form! For example, the other day I had just finished a reading, when almost as a PS I was shown a dart. I could have ignored that as silly, but when I asked my sitter if she could understand why I would be shown a dart, she laughed and explained that her husband had been captain of his regional darts team! The whole point is that you have to trust that these things are communications from Spirit! At first you tend to think that they are your own thoughts, and it is difficult to disassociate them from Spirit communication, but I say again, it's all about trust."

People are individuals and while some folk will find what they are looking for within the arms of the spiritualist church, it is by no means the only pathway to rekindling and developing one's own mediumship. One very useful tool is the act and the art of meditation because before one can hear words uttered from another realm, one needs to learn how to be still. How to be quiet. How to listen.

Learning how to listen is not always easy because the truth of the matter is that we all like the sound of our voices a tad too much, but learning how to meditate, which is the first step along the pathway of learning how to listen, is not nearly as difficult as you might imagine and not nearly as difficult as some people might like you to believe that it is.

To illustrate my point, a few years ago there were huge numbers of schools and individuals offering to teach Transcendental Meditation (TM) and for this three- or four-day course they would demand many hundreds of pounds. And yet the truth of the matter is that the "course", which was stretched out to three or four days, obviously in an attempt to justify the ludicrous fees, could have been taught in less than a morning or an afternoon to any student with half a thinking brain. The Maharishi Yogi's and Sai Baba's of this world have a lot to answer for!

And yet, whichever discipline of meditation you employ,

it must be said that the routine of sitting comfortably in a safe environment for 20 minutes every day, closing your eyes and directing your mind to whatever state of relaxation you can attain, is a wonderful short cut to a place where contact with another world is possible.

The idea is to empty the mind of all conscious thought and this is incredibly difficult to do. The TM system revolves around the repetitive chant of a mantra while Buddhist tradition is to concentrate on a single object – the Lotus flower being the favourite symbol of the faith. Those coming to meditation for the first time will say that it impossible to clear the mind – that there are always thoughts dashing into the brain such as the latest electricity bill, the car's wobbly front wheel, the kids' terrible school reports, that worrying lump you've suddenly found, the last nasty argument you had with your best friend or your husband/wife/son/daughter/boss – and the skill is to absorb these thoughts and let them wash over you while the mind detaches from reality. It *can* be difficult and it *does* take some practice to master the technique, but it is most certainly not impossible and the benefits are quite profound. Like riding a bike, the technique once learned is never forgotten.

Once you have acquired the basic technique of meditation, it is quite feasible to go into that meditative state, not reciting mantras or concentrating on symbols like the Lotus flower or whatever, but simply thinking of the person who has passed over that you would like to communicate with. Holding that person in your thoughts will bring images and memories to mind of times you shared with them when they were alive in this realm, and providing you are patient, sooner or later you will start hearing messages.

You may hear them as words, either spoken aloud or whispered in your ear, or you may simply experience silent communication through the process of pictures and thought forms. Either way, this communication is valid and should not be dismissed as imagination. However *do be patient* because it can take quite a while, sometimes weeks and months, to work up to this state of psychic awareness and in this modern helter skelter world where everything is so immediate, people get easily bored and fall by the wayside.

Think of learning to meditate in the same way you might think of leaning to speak a foreign language. If you give up after the first couple of weeks you might just manage *"Una café con leche, por favor"* but stick at it and the joy of speaking in another tongue becomes more ardent and enjoyable with every passing month.

Another very well proven technique which is guaranteed to enhance your clairvoyant abilities is learning how to remember your dreams.

As Sandy has already explained, when we are asleep and dreaming, we are in an altered state and it is in this altered state that we are able to close the gap between our own souls here on planet earth and the souls of our departed loved ones who have moved on to that other realm that some men call Heaven.

In the early days of my exploration into the world of spirit, I got into the habit of going to bed with a note pad and a pen on my bedside table and as soon as I woke from the dream I would scribble what I could remember of it down on the pad. In the early days there were just a few isolated words and half garbled sentences but gradually over the months I found I was remembering more and more until after a year or so I had virtually total recall of my dream state journeys and adventures.

I got so good at this that towards the end of the second year of record keeping I found that I could get into my bed at the end of the day, meditate for a few minutes, and pre-programme my dreams to take me to wherever I wanted to go, to talk to and be with anyone I wanted to be with. If this sounds a bit farfetched, let me assure you that anyone with a practical interest in the paranormal can achieve this state of self-discipline.

In my case, the results were quite spectacular but I found that there was a price to pay for all this psychic activity. First of all, it was tempting to live for those hours of slumber to the extent that one's hours of wakefulness became empty and exhausted; the dream state began to dominate the reality of my life and my life became the poorer for it. My healthy mental attitude became tarnished with arrogance and ambition, especially when I found that not only could one make contact with the dead, one could also make contact with the living and impinge oneself into *their* dreams, to the extent of being able to influence some of their waking actions.

This was very dangerous ground and once I realized what was happening I backed off rather quickly. It has to be said in my defence that at that time I was studying other aspects of the paranormal that were less than wholly spiritual in their nature and had I kept to the purely "spiritual" pathway I'm certain that I would have made a lot more progress than I did.

Things like the Tarot cards and the I Ching are, at first glance, a million miles away from spiritualism, and yet they are both disciplines whereby the more you work with them the more you open the psychic doorways of the mind. Therefore, without setting yourself up as a 'Gypsy Jim' or a 'Madam Ping Pong', the study of both the Tarot and I Ching is an exercise in spiritual expansion and can be used as such without any other agenda. It's a bit like learning Latin at school. You're never going to use the language but it's a great mental discipline.

Without falling into the "you are what you eat" cliché, it must be said that a healthy body is useful in support of the enquiring mind. Excessive fatty food, alcohol and tobacco all clog the senses and should be avoided. Big meals that leave you feeling stodgy and bloated should be skipped in favour of lighter meals of smaller portions. This diet is not advocated as a weight loss programme but as a method of avoiding a build-up of toxins within the physical body and to maintain sound physical health.

Sandy, you may recall, has suffered with MS for many years and yet through the regime of this power diet combined with a bit of PMA she has kept herself mobile and out of her wheel chair. She points out that it is much easier to maintain a positive mental attitude when you are trim and fit than it is when you are fat and sluggish.

Unfortunately some of us, myself included, will never be slim; it's in the genes and there's very little we can do about it... But one way or the other, we have to combat that state of sluggishness and it rests within our own hands to use whatever means are at our disposal to achieve this goal. To say that a sluggish body equates with a sluggish mind is a bit of an over simplification, but there's more than just a grain of truth in it.

Finally, and this might be an odd question to ask, but why would you actually *want* to develop your own psychic gifts and clairvoyant abilities?

As any medium will tell you, it is not always an easy pathway to travel and there are pit falls and problems that other people always seem to be able to avoid that cling to clairvoyants like sphagnum moss. I've never met a medium of whom it could be said they'd had an easy life and every medium I have met seems to have suffered more than their fair share of drama and trauma throughout life. Spirit seems to take perverse pleasure in its choice of servants, avoiding the strong, the hale, the hearty and the healthy, inevitably in favour of the weak and dispossessed who seem to start life at the very bottom of the social ladder and have to fight rung by bloody rung for survival. There are a couple of notable exceptions such as Daniel Dunglas Home, the Victorian spiritualist and levitator, and one acknowledges the likes of Madame Blavatsky and Arthur Conan Doyle, who while profoundly interested in spiritualism were not themselves mediums. Generally speaking, while the "upper" classes have always enjoyed a healthy interest in the subject, the clairvoyants and mediums usually tend to come from ordinary working class backgrounds.

If we take Sandy as an example, no one could have had a less promising start in life, and her early years through childhood into teens were filled with drama followed by crisis – and yet through adulthood to the present time she has always been regarded as an excellent medium, and now with the arrival of her spirit guide Leo, she is beginning to be recognised as one of the leading psychic artists in the whole of the country… Who would have thought that this might be possible on those days she struggled up the hill outside her home in Derbyshire, weeping in fear and frustration while carrying a child across the icy tracks of the High Peaks? Certainly not Sandy herself.

Having a degree of psychic ability can be a double edged sword. On the plus side, if you are able to reach into the psyche of a fellow human being and bring them some encouragement with the information you are able to glean from the world of spirit, you harm none and help many. On the other side of the coin, it's not a lot of fun when you suddenly realize that your partner or your boyfriend/girlfriend is telling you lies.

What do you do? Challenge them without any evidence other than your psychic awareness, or remain silent and suffer in solitude? How do you feel when you see someone you love moving into danger and you can't do anything to help them because your warnings are ignored?

Being clairvoyant can enhance your social life. You get invited to a lot of parties. The trouble is, you're invited for what you can do not for who you are. Times without number I've been invited to a "do" and have been encouraged to take my Tarot cards. Sandy sometimes has the same problem with her sketch bad and poor old Steve Holbrook can't go anywhere without being crammed into a corner by a horde of people all wanting a private reading or a pearl of wisdom.

And I think there is one other thing to remember. Those people who are genuinely clairvoyant with the powers of mediumship will always see themselves as the servants of Spirit and, as such, sometimes their lives are their own, and sometimes their lives are *not* their own.

I came into contact with my first medium when I was only 14 years old and that is now 50 years ago. Since then I have met many mediums, some good, some bad, some totally brilliant, but when I think about it, I do not know of a single medium who has not paid a very high price for the privilege of serving the world of spirit.

Twelve: Conclusions

As you may recall, I first met Sandy at The Marriott Hotel in Portsmouth back in 2009. At that time I was impressed by the accuracy of some of her sketches and described them as having a simplistic and naïve quality. I failed to realize that this was one of Sandy's very first public exhibitions and when, only a couple of weeks ago, I saw her again over in the West Yorkshire town of Keighley, I immediately recognised that her talents had moved on in leaps and bounds over the intervening three years. Her pictures were significantly more detailed and had lost much of their simplistic naiveté. She worked with greater speed, frequently using both hands at the same time, producing, on average, a different portrait every 10 minutes. One could call these portraits "sketches" but it would be doing them an injustice. They were highly detailed drawings that would have made any professional artist jealous and, indeed, a friend of mine who *is* a professional artist has freely admitted that it would take him "half a day to come up with anything like that."

We must place this comment in context with the fact that Sandy has never had any formal training as an artist and on the one occasion when she did try to benefit from a few lessons, her "teacher" gave up on her in disgust after less than half a dozen sessions.

On the evening of the Keighley demonstration I was also acutely aware of the interest Sandy attracted from her audience; they may have been listening to the clairvoyant's words but their eyes were glued to the overhead screen that magnified and illuminated Sandy's works in progress.

Speaking as one who has attended many hundreds of demonstrations, I found that the act of watching an artist draw the face of the spirit that was being channeled by the medium to be a unique and fascinating experience. I wondered why it had never been done before and felt that it wouldn't be a bad idea if every other medium out there on the circuit spent a little bit of time going in pursuit of their own psychic artist.

Sandy's presence certainly brought another dimension to Stephen Holbrook's evening and seemed to give him the inspiration to deliver one of the most poignant demonstrations of clairvoyance I'd ever seen him give – and I was "on the road" with him for 11 years, remember!

Another subtle string to Sandy's bow is her increasing ability to come up with images of spirit guides and an ever-growing number of people, including professional mediums, are approaching her with this commission. This isn't really surprising because Man is quintessentially a curious animal, intrigued and frustrated by mystery and sometimes even fearful of it. Nevertheless, there is an overriding desire to *know* – to discover the secret of life and as part of that quest, if he is to understand it, what lies beyond death.

People die.

We see it in the newspapers and on our TV screens every day. And yet, the dead bodies in the dust bowls of Afghanistan or the flood victims in Bangladesh remain disassociated and impersonal to us. We say the right words and make the right sounds of sympathy, but the truth is that we really have no perception of what it might be like to be a starving child in Africa or a dying baby ravaged with malnutrition and HIV. We have become inured and anaesthetized by the media images that have bombarded our senses for the last 40 years and the best we can do to salve our consciences is to drop a few quid into the Oxfam or Save The Children buckets when they are waved under our noses.

But it's not the same, is it, when one of our own loved ones dies – a father, a mother, a daughter or a son? *Then* we feel and react very differently. This is up close and personal. This is *our* loss, *our* tragedy... We are devastated and bereaved and in that bereavement lose sight of the fact that while we might be burying our loved one in Chipping Norton or Great Yarmouth, a million other families all over the world are burying their own loved ones somewhere else – and there were a million who did it the day before and there will be another million who will do it the day after.

We focus on the personal aspects of our loss and fail to put death into perspective – and the perspective is that death is just as much a part of the life experience as is the birth process. It's as natural as birthdays, bonfires, engagements, weddings and divorces. They don't lump "births, deaths and marriages" under one banner for nothing!

It is hard to think of this when you're standing at the graveside watching your favourite Granny pushing up the daisies, but if one could, then it would help the grieving process and one always needs to be mindful that things could be worse.

That's your Granny down there in that quiet English grave. She lived a good life, kept most of her own teeth, saw half a dozen strapping grandchildren, was well loved by her family and was cosseted by the NHS... She died in her sleep with a smile on her face. She could have been a hungry 12-year-old girl, raped by a brigade of Taliban, mutilated by axes and finished off with half a dozen bullets from an AK47. Oh yes, things *could* be a *lot* worse!

If one can believe in an afterlife there need be no fear of death – and actually, I reckon if you did a straw poll, not that many people would admit to being afraid of death although we all might admit to being fearful of the actual process of dying – and even if you find the idea of post mortem survival a difficult pill to swallow, common sense dictates that we all have to die sometime, so why waste one's precious hours of life worrying

about the inevitable? Furthermore, even if you have no spiritual leanings at all whatsoever, but presuming you do have just a
smidgen of intelligence, then surely your *common sense* must tell
you that there is some form of life after death.

You could argue that rather than being created, Man
evolved, but through that process of evolution his spirit has also
evolved into being a higher intellectual energy with the power
and ability to reason. Even if we go back to our Neanderthal and
Cro-Magnon ancestors, it is clear from their cave paintings that
they believed in an afterlife, and that belief has filtered down
through every culture in every part of the world since Homo sa-
piens discovered the secret of walking on two legs.

You could argue that Man needs religion – needs to believe in the existence of something greater than himself – and
maybe there is some truth in this because what would be the im-
plication of there *not* being anything after death? What happens
if there is not an afterlife and when we die the light simply goes
out and that's that?

Were that to be the case then it flies in the face of world
history, the history and traditions of every culture that has ever
drawn breath on this planet; it makes a mockery of our human
achievements in the realms of art, medicine and philosophy, and
it actually makes a mockery of our very humanity and every human thought and feeling we have ever experienced, both as individuals and as a species. More importantly it goes against the
grain of every scrap of *evidence* that has ever been gathered, recorded and collated since the beginning of time and the invention
of language. What are some people so afraid of that they cannot
accept the logic of the obvious?

In the great scheme of things, I think this is where people
like Sandy Ingham have an extremely important role to play.

If Sandy, through her mediumship and her artwork can alleviate some of the fear of dying, if she can help strip away some

of the mystery, then in my opinion she does the world a great service. If the fear of death and dying can be removed then how much more vital and enjoyable our lives could be!

The church condemns spiritualism and, in the most ludicrous piece of contrariness, instructs its congregations to ignore the evidence provided by spiritualists and mediums for a spiritual afterlife. It tells us that all we need to do is have blind faith in the church's word.

At the other end of the spectrum, science, in denial of the same evidence, simply makes itself look arrogant and foolish.

To me these attitudes seem positively criminal and I cannot help but wonder what might happen if the church committed some of its enormous fiscal wealth and science dedicated some open-minded effort into researching the mystery and the phenomena of communication with the spirit world. If this could happen, what a different and better world we might create.

Many spiritualists that I have spoken with are delighted by this thought and would be willing and eager to commit themselves to such a programme of experimentation.

They realize, with prescient clairvoyance, just what a profound difference this would make, not only to society's view of all faiths and all religions, but also in changing the attitudes *within* and *between* faiths. It would remove conflict and suspicion and would generate love and understanding within the heart of Man for his fellow men. This really would be the Christian "second coming" and the true dawning of The Aquarian Age. Working together towards an open, honest and spiritual society could be the saving grace for all Mankind. The Spirit is willing, and now it's up to The Pope and Albert Einstein.

***

The Otherside Press is a division of and serves as the main public education and communication vehicle for the **American Association for Standards in Mediumship and Psychical Investigation, Inc. (ASSMPI),** adhering to the ASSMPI standards for truth and reliability as an authoritative source for information regarding ongoing research into and evidence of survival beyond death.

The mission of The Otherside Press is to publish and deliver afterlife educational books and publications, Including paranormal research and certain spiritual publications in keeping with the direction and modus operandi of the ASSMPI and its Subsidiary groups and organizations. ASSMPI is an independent international association run as a non-profit organization to help maintain standards within the industry and to investigate all forms of mediumship.

The ASSMPI is committed to raising the standards of mediumship and connecting a registered community of professional and like-minded individuals who either work in this field or desire to enhance and expand their knowledge and professionalism within mediumship and its associated practice and deployment.

By educating the public that death is not the end of existence, and by emphasizing that neither is it the domain of religion or superstition, nor is it incompatible with scientific surety, we engage the public to learn to recognize and accept the continued efforts of people who have died, working on in spirit to communicate the life-affirming message that death is not an ending, but a natural step into the next stage of life.

A U.S.-registered 501(c)(3) charity, the ASSMPI has a three-pronged approach to sharing the evidence of life after death with the public.

1. The Otherside Press Books strive to bring into print and keep in print the most important contemporary writings, as well as some of the historically most important writings that bring forth the truth of Spirit (http://www.tospbooks.com)

2. The Otherside Press magazine offers articles and timely information on the evidence of survival beyond death. The Otherside Press Magazine is a labor of love, inspired by spirit to serve. As the main communications arm of the ASSMPI, we at The Otherside Press Magazine work as volunteers to serve others by sharing the message that life does not end at death. We encourage you to share your story, your experience with The Other Side, too (http://www.theothersidepress.com)

3. The ASSMPI Spirit and Science Journal (ASSJ) publishes peer-reviewed scientific research papers dealing with many different aspects of the afterlife and the paranormal. For professional researchers in afterlife science and paranormal subject matter, the Journal features substantive reports on all aspects of afterlife research and other avenues of paranormal science. (http://afterlifesciencejournal.com)

CPSIA information can be obtained
at www.ICGtesting.com
Printed in the USA
FFOW03n0035181017
41251FF